Table of Contents:

ACKNOWLEDGEMENTS

I would like to thank sincerely those people who cheerfully assisted me in my research for this book. Unfortunately there just are too many to thank individually but I am indebted to the clergy, churchwardens, sextons and parishioners who met me at the church gate and also to those who responded to my requests, by letter, email and telephone, for information.

There are, however, a few whose assistance was such that I do need to name them. They are: David Higgins of Easkey; the Very Revd. Arfon Williams, Dean of Elphin, who gave me a copy of an unpublished history of Knocknarea; Thomas Pearson of Meenglass who provided information, unavailable elsewhere, about the church which was demolished in 1961; Dr. David Butler and Julian C. Walton who pointed me to the sources of information about former churches in the Dioceses of Emly, Lismore and Waterford; Dermot Mulligan, Carlow Co. Museum, and Eamon Browne, Kerry Co. Library, who assisted in tracing photographs; Canon Gary Dowd, former Rector of Carlow Union; Revd. Dr. Adrian Empey for writing the foreword: Dr. Raymond Refausse, Dr. Susan Hood and Mrs Mary Furlong of the RCB Library who were most patient and helpful during my search for information in the sources of the library.

Finally I wish to thank my wife, Sheila, and Simon Walker, a fellow enthusiast for church architecture, for reading the text and removing the infelicities of language and terminology. Those which remain are my responsibility.

SOURCES OF ILLUSTRATIONS

Unless stated otherwise, the illustrations are by the author. The remaining illustrations are reproduced by kind permission of the following people and institutions, or come from the following published sources:

Annestown, elevation and plans by J. Pain from *Architectural Drawings, Ms 138 6/1*, by kind permission of the Representative Church Body of Church of Ireland; Blennerville, photographs from p. 81, *Blennerville: Gateway to Tralee's Past*, Kelly, L., Lucid, G. and O'Sullivan, M., Tralee 1989 (permission sought from Blennerville Windmill Company); Belfast Parish Church, engraving by Bruce and Nelson from *Twenty-One Views in Belfast and Its Neighbourhood*, ed. P.D.Hardy, Dublin, 1837, by kind permission of the Linen Hall Library, Belfast and the Ulster Architectural Heritage Society; Carlow, from the archives and by kind permission of the Carlow Historical and Archaeological Society; Drumglass Old Parish Church, by kind permission of the Rector and Select Vestry of Drumglass Parish Church; Dublin, St. Ann's Dawson Street, line drawing of the design for the west front by T.N. Deane from *The Irish Builder*, October, 1868; photograph of the Evie Hone cartoon of St. Anne by kind permission of the Rector and Select Vestry of St. Ann's Parish Church, Dublin; Dublin, St. Audoen's, drawing of fresco from *The Irish Builder*, March 1887; Meenglass, line drawing by Welland and Gillespie from *Miscellaneous Architectural Drawings, Portfolio 25*, by kind permission of the Representative Church Body of the Church of Ireland.

I have much pleasure in commending this unusual study of churches dedicated in honour of St Anne partly for sentimental reasons as a former vicar of St Ann's, Dublin, but more particularly because of the eccentric disregard for historical or theological considerations that such a choice of dedication might have aroused in the sensibilities of an earlier age!

None of which is to enter a protest. The practice of venerating 'saints' reaches far back into the history of the church. Indeed, St Luke's treatment of the martyrdom of Stephen in the Acts of the Apostles seems clearly to be inspired by the crucifixion narrative. Hebrews places considerable weight on the 'great cloud of witnesses'. The persecutions suffered by generations of early Christians yielded a rich harvest of martyrs, who were naturally venerated by their communities. Like their pagan neighbours, Christians commemorated the anniversaries of those who died confessing their faith. When the Peace of the Church finally arrived with the reign of Constantine at the beginning of the fourth century, it became possible to build churches either on the site of the martyr's grave, or else through the translation of relics to a church located elsewhere. Eusebius, the great church historian and contemporary of the Council of Nicaea, tells us how the peace produced a spate of 'dedication ceremonies in the cities and consecrations of newly built places of worship' [History of the Church 10:3], and supplies the dedication speech for the cathedral of Tyre in 314.

That such practices gave rise to much theological speculation was, in the nature of things, inevitable. The ancient creeds speak of the 'communion of saints', though what was intended by the phrase is far from certain. But what was the role of the saints in the economy of the redemptive purposes of God? Were they merely 'role models', to use contemporary language? Or could they be conduits of intercession in virtue of their merit and miraculous attestations? While such issues were hotly debated by medieval theologians, they naturally attracted the attention of our Christocentric, not to say bibliocentric, Protestant forbears. Their reaction to the vast literature of medieval hagiography might be said to be enough to cause a serious theological rash. Suffice to say, that The Book of Common Prayer says it all: only saints with a specific biblical credentials or renowned Irish saints warrant inclusion in Red Letter days of liturgical observance.

Given such reservations, it is astonishing that a considerable number of our parish churches were dedicated in the course of the eighteenth and nineteenth centuries to the completely fictitious mother of the Blessed Virgin Mary. What this intriguing study reveals is nothing less than a complete disregard for such fine distinctions on the part of our church-building ancestors in the course of the past two centuries in particular. If it is possible to risk a generalisation on the basis of the following study, it would seem that non-theological considerations were uppermost in the minds of the patrons. In the eighteenth century, Queen Anne features prominently as a probable reason for assigning such dedications. In the following century the desire to commemorate a wife or mother by a generous patron seems to be the dominant consideration. Those tender consciences that might in other circumstances be disturbed by the dedication of churches to apocryphal saints may, however, relax. No apostasy was intended. The original intention of dedicating St Anne's, Belfast, in honour of St Patrick was quietly dropped as a consequence of the underwriting of the building by the Marquis of Donegall, whose first wife was Anne, daughter of the Duke of Hamilton. When, in 1841, a committee of conservatives raised some funds to present to Colonel Bruen of Oak Park, Carlow, after his unexpected election victory, the good colonel decided to put the money instead to the building of a free church in Carlow dedicated to St Anne, almost certainly by way of honouring his wife, Anne Wandesforde.

Far from denouncing such manoeuvres, we ought rather to rejoice in the variety of parochial heritage, whether Norman, Plantation, Georgian, First Fruits, or Neo-Gothic. The parish church by its very nature is rooted in the life of the communities that gave birth to them. Eccentricity is part and parcel of such a rich heritage. Ancient churchyards, bespeak of the lives and loves of countless generations for whom the parish church marked the rites of passage from birth to death. The church, in its successive reconstructions, stands as a witness in stone to the sacramental bond that connects so many centuries, cultures, not to mention theologies. It is only fitting that such buildings should express their individuality and their participation in the seamless communion of saints by virtue of their dedication in honour of the saints, whether biblical, local, or even legendary. All are hallowed by the lives of those who lived within the ancient parochial borders. If all this needs a theological gloss, one need look no farther than Gray's Elegy in a Country Churchyard:

> *Here rests his head upon the lap of Earth*
> *A youth to Fortune and to Fame unknown.*
> *Fair Science frowned not on his humble birth,*
> *And Melancholy marked him for her own.*
>
> *No farther seek his merits to disclose,*
> *Or draw his frailties from their dread abode*
> *(There they alike in trembling hope repose),*
> *The bosom of his Father and his God.*

Adrian Empey

INTRODUCTION

Over the past few decades there has been a growth of interest in the built environment and awareness of the need to preserve that heritage. As a result of my research for this book, however, I have come to believe that there is an urgent need for members of the Church of Ireland to be more aware of, and value, the built heritage of their church: not just the small number of famous well documented buildings but also the little known churches in remote areas. It is my hope that this publication will stimulate others to provide a record of many more of what have been described as modest architectural treasures which are testaments to the complexity of Irish life and grace the areas in which they stand.

The search for information about the buildings, dedicated to St. Anne has been a mixed experience. It was rewarding, even inspiring at times, to visit what were clearly cherished churches and exciting to discover some which deserve to be much more widely known. It was frustrating however to find so little information about many of them and particularly those smaller remote buildings. Keeping and preserving records of a large proportion of its built heritage appears unfortunately to have had a very low priority throughout the history of our church. During the twentieth century record keeping appears to have permitted some churches to descend into virtual oblivion with little record of their existence being kept even to the point where there are no written details or photographs of their closure.

In his major study of Gothic Revival architecture in Ireland, Richardson expresses the same frustration, lamenting the dearth of studies of Church of Ireland architectural history, the disappearance of many buildings without record, the limited number of written records which were kept or have survived and the absence of photographic records. Sadly, the history and architecture of too many churches has not been chronicled by church, diocese or parish but was left to interested and enthusiastic architectural, clerical and local historians and parishioners. Much of what is known about churches has depended on those individuals and it is to them that this book is dedicated.

Our built heritage is a major asset to the church and an important part of the environment and history of the country which ought to be recorded. This is a crucial task which should not depend solely upon the efforts and interests of enthusiasts. There is an evident need for an officer within church administration whose responsibilities include the promotion of greater awareness of the history and architecture of churches through publications and exhibitions and the provision of guidance for parishes and dioceses in what should be the obligatory making and keeping of full photographic and written records.

ST. ANNE

Nothing is known about the parents of the Blessed Virgin Mary. They are not mentioned in the New Testament or in contemporary primary sources. The Gospels say little of the life of Mary so it is not surprising that they are silent about her mother or father. A very ancient tradition, however, names Joachim and Anne as the parents of Mary but St. Anne is a 'constructed' saint whose history was created by the early church to fill perceived gaps in the biblical narrative.

The earliest document in which the story of Anne is told is the apocryphal Protoevangelium of James, circa AD 150. Although not recognised by the early church as being inspired, it was influential and had great authority in the Eastern Church in Jerusalem and Syria. The story of her life follows the Old Testament paradigm of mothers, such as Hannah, mother of Samuel, and Elisabeth, mother of John the Baptist, whose long years of barrenness were followed by divine intervention resulting in the birth of a child pledged to the service of God. Anne's 'constructed' life strongly resembles that of Hannah, a Greek name meaning grace, which became Anna in the Latin tongue.

According to tradition Joachim, a Levite priest in some sources, and Anne were a pious but childless couple living in Nazareth. On a feast day Joachim was prevented from entering the temple by a man named Reuben because, according to him, men without children were unworthy to be admitted to that holy place. Joachim retired to the desert for forty days to fast, pray and meditate while Anne mourned her barrenness at home in Nazareth. Both Joachim and Anne were visited by angels and, in due time, their daughter, Mary, was born.

The first record of St. Anne outside Jerusalem and Syria is the dedication to her, circa 565 AD, of a church built by Emperor Justinian I in Constantinople. By the early eighth century her name was included in the liturgies of the Western Church and relics in Rome date from the same period. The cult of St. Anne may have been brought westwards by refugees fleeing from Moslem conquests in the Eastern Mediterranean. During the eighth and ninth centuries St. Anne appeared increasingly in pictorial religious art in the Western Church represented there with the infant Mary in her arms.

The Protoevangelium of James was not accepted by the Western Church until its contents were included by Jacobus de Voragine in his 'Golden Legend' in the thirteenth century. This Byzantine work is a collection of the lives of saints and short studies of Christian festivals. It presents a sequence of scenes from the lives of Anne and Joachim commencing with their meeting at the Golden Gate. From this time, the story and cult associated with St Anne spread over Western Europe until she became one of the most popular saints in the mediaeval Western Church. The first dedication of a church in England to St. Anne, which took place in 1227, is evidence of that spread westwards. St Anne continued to be an important figure in pictorial religious art throughout the mediaeval period, still represented with the infant Mary in her arms but increasingly portrayed teaching a slightly older Mary to read. She was also a prominent figure in Florentine art from the mid-fourteenth century onwards.

The spread and growth of her cult was fostered further by the soldiers returning from the Crusades. Supposed relics of the saint, such as her veil which is in Apt Cathedral in France, were brought from the Holy Land. The feast of St. Anne, celebrated from a much earlier time on continental Europe, was ordered, by the Pope, to be observed in England in 1382 probably in association with the marriage of Richard II to Anne of Bohemia. Her feast day became an important communal celebration marked by popular devotional practices, water rites at holy wells and mediaeval street theatre. She also became the patron saint of many mediaeval guilds.

The cult was given authority by theological discussions and controversy about whether Anne had immaculately conceived Mary and whether she had married three times, a theory called the 'trinubium'. According to this, Anne married Cleopas after the death of Joachim and then on the death of Cleopas, she married Salome. In these marriages it was believed she had become the grandmother of Jesus' cousins, some of whom were later to become His disciples. Another tradition suggests that Anne was one of three daughters of Mattan, a priest who lived at Bethlehem. One of these sisters, named Mary was the grandmother of two disciples while the other sister, named Sobe, was the grandmother of John the Baptist.

The high point of the cult was in the early sixteenth century but a reaction to the excesses attached to it set in at the Reformation. Martin Luther [1485-1546], whose vow on becoming a monk had been made to St. Anne, attacked both the religious practices, such as those associated with the guilds dedicated to her, and the social practices attached to the cult. Henry VIII dissolved the guilds and took possession of their chantry chapels in England in 1547. Decisions made by the Roman Catholic Church at the Council of Trent [1545-1563] also reduced the status of her feast day on the continent.

There is some evidence that the practice of the cult of St Anne was brought to Ireland by Anglo-Norman settlers and soldiers. The oldest known record of the dedication of a building to St. Anne in Ireland is that of the private oratory at Passage East, in the parish of Kill St. Nicholas, Co. Waterford in

1284. It eventually became the parish church and then later passed to the Church of Ireland at the Reformation. It is possible that other medieval churches such as Mallow, Co. Cork, founded slightly earlier in the early twelfth century according to some sources, may have been given the same dedication although no record of that has survived.

An unknown number of holy wells were dedicated to St. Anne when her cult arrived in England and, somewhat later, in Ireland. A visit to the well was an important part of the celebrations and devotions on the saint's feast day but also by many throughout the year. As in other areas of popular religious devotion, various excesses of behaviour developed which were disapproved of by the Roman Catholic Church and the cult of the holy well slowly declined.

Only two wells dedicated to St. Anne were recorded on the original Ordnance Survey Maps of Ireland, circa 1833, and both were close to churches dedicated to her at Passage East, Co. Waterford, and Killane, Co.Wexford. There is now no trace of the well at Passage East and the water source must have been diverted elsewhere but the well at Killane is still visited by pilgrims as shown by the various votive offerings, many modern in nature, around the well.

Churches are built to the Glory of God and in many cases dedicated in honour of a saint, or occasionally two saints, although some are dedicated to a religious concept, e.g. the Holy Trinity, or an event, e.g. the Annunciation, the Epiphany and the Nativity. The earliest recorded example of the dedication of a church to a saint is dated AD 314. The practice of dedication was seen as a way of helping to make them holy places, separated from unworthy or secular use.

Brandon writes in his book on Church of Ireland dedications that 'it is fitting we should dedicate our churches to great men and women of God because they direct our thoughts to lives devoted to the service of God .... [and] whose memory we uphold' in this way. It would seem, however, that in the mid-1950s in the Church of Ireland the practice of dedication of its churches to saints was not widespread with more than half of the churches being known simply by the name of the parish, village, townland or small town in which they stood. Being a largely rural country those names may have sufficed to distinguish churches whereas in the comparatively few large towns and cities dedicating a church was useful as it provided each church with an identity. Perhaps there was also a slight element of Protestant reaction to the role of saints in the Roman Catholic Church.

It is possible however that the records of some dedications may have been lost. The vast majority of Church of Ireland churches are post-Reformation and it is almost certain that deeds of consecration would have contained the names of the saints, if any, to whom they were dedicated. Unfortunately, few deeds appear to have survived. Together with other church records, many deeds probably perished in 1922 in the fire at the Public Record Office, Dublin, during the Irish Civil War.

The records in the Irish Church Directory in the mid-1950s show that churches were dedicated to a total of 139 saints, of whom only thirteen are known with certainty to be women. Something is known of the lives of well known saints from both Biblical times and the days of the early church but there is little documentary evidence of their lives while others, such as St. Patrick, can be the subject of academic disagreement. Most of the saints named in Church of Ireland dedications come from the age of the Celtic Church and their lives are poorly documented. With the passage of time most are obscure, surrounded by myth or legend, completely lost in antiquity or difficult or impossible to identify accurately even, in some cases, to the point of not knowing the saint's gender. Many were associated with only one parish and their names may also have been changed or corrupted through time especially where no official records were kept or had survived.

Prior to the Reformation many dedications throughout the Western Church were changed and replaced by the names of more fashionable or politically expedient saints. Virtually all dedications to St Thomas of Canterbury were renamed St. Thomas the Apostle during the reign of Henry VIII to whom recognition of Thomas Becket's memory was unacceptable. In more recent times the dedications of two Church of Ireland buildings to Saint Anne were changed. Dedications to the saint were not retained when the new Dunhill Parish Church was built at Annestown, Diocese of Lismore, in 1857 and when Enniskillen Parish Church, Diocese of Clogher, gained cathedral status in 1923.

Of churches in the Church of Ireland dedicated to women, seventy-eight were named St. Mary, in honour of the Blessed Virgin Mary, and the next most frequent dedication to a women was to St. Anne [Ann in certain churches] who is traditionally believed to have been the mother of the Virgin Mary. Of the twenty-eight dedications to St. Anne, six, and possibly two others, were from mediaeval times. Of the others, which were dedicated between c.1619 and 1911, three appear to remember Queen Anne and eight are most likely in memory of loved ones central to the lives of those who played a major role in the building of the churches.

In pre-Reformation times every church had a patronal festival. If there was no dedication, the festival was held on the anniversary of the date of consecration of the church. For those churches with a dedication, the festival was usually held on the Saint's feast day in the Liturgical Calendar of the Church. The Church of Ireland, however, does not make liturgical provision for the feast day of St. Anne on 26 July. The 1926 Book of Common Prayer included twenty saints in the calendar, to which were added three, St. Brigid, St. Columba and St. Mary Magdalene, in the Alternative Prayer Book of 1984 and a further three, St. Joseph of Nazareth, St. Philip Deacon and St. James, the Brother of Our Lord, in the Book of Common Prayer, 2004.

It would appear that, in the absence of liturgical provision, the saint's feast day is not marked in those churches dedicated to her. Decoration of the churches in glass or stone to reflect their dedication to the saint is also limited being found in just three buildings. There are stained glass windows depicting her in Drumglass Parish Church and in St. Ann's, Dawson Street, Dublin. The latter church also holds a cartoon of the saint by Evie Hone, the renowned Dublin stained glass artist, but the window was not commissioned. The only representation in stone is at St. Anne's Cathedral, Belfast, where the saint is one of four female figures carved on the tympanum above the main portal on the west front.

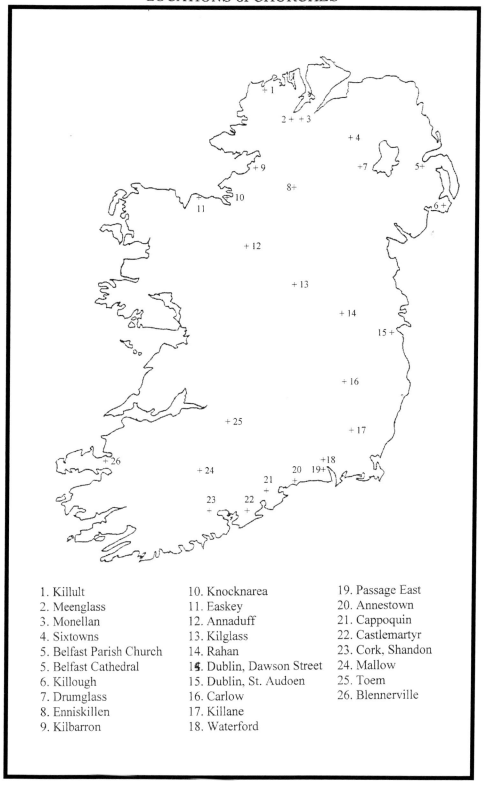

1. Killult
2. Meenglass
3. Monellan
4. Sixtowns
5. Belfast Parish Church
5. Belfast Cathedral
6. Killough
7. Drumglass
8. Enniskillen
9. Kilbarron

10. Knocknarea
11. Easkey
12. Annaduff
13. Kilglass
14. Rahan
14. Dublin, Dawson Street
15. Dublin, St. Audoen
16. Carlow
17. Killane
18. Waterford

19. Passage East
20. Annestown
21. Cappoquin
22. Castlemartyr
23. Cork, Shandon
24. Mallow
25. Toem
26. Blennerville

ANNADUFF: ST. ANN

St. Ann's Parish Church, Annaduff [Eanagh Dubh : the black marsh], in the Diocese of Ardagh, is situated close to the River Shannon, some five miles south east of Carrick-on-Shannon, Co. Leitrim. There is a tradition that St. Patrick and his followers crossed the Shannon at this place and, journeying on, spread Christianity to the West of Ireland.

The present parish church stands close to the ruins of an ancient parish church said to have been built on the site of an abbey founded in AD 766. The church was listed in the Register of Clonmacnoise and there are records of Vicars of Annaduff from 1412. The ancient church was still roofed and in use until the present church was consecrated for worship. It was described at that date as a rectangular building of limestone with quoins, a modernised doorway and a fifteenth century window with crockets. There is a local tradition that the bell of the ancient church was buried nearby to prevent Cromwell's army using the metal to make weapons.

The building of the new church began in 1815 when a grant of £1600 was received from the Board of First Fruits. Built to accommodate 300, the church was consecrated on 3 December 1820 although work, such as the installation in 1825 of a bell inscribed 'Clarke, Ringsend Foundry, Dublin, 1824', a clock in 1826, seats in the gallery and completion of the churchyard wall and gates, continued for a few years. It was dedicated to St. Ann but there is no extant record to indicate if the dedication was passed on from the ancient parish church and there is nothing in church or local records around 1820 to suggest a possible reason for the name chosen.

The church, described in 1837 as being in 'later English style', is of typical early nineteenth century Board of First Fruits design with a three-bay rectangular hall and integrated west tower of rubble with roughcast harling. The openings on the building are pointed and all have dressed stone surrounds and hood mouldings. The comparatively generous loan permitted the architect to provide some decorative features mainly on the south side which faced the course of the old main road from Sligo to Dublin. The modern road now runs some distance to the east and out of sight of the church.

As in many churches of that period and design there are no openings on the north wall, probably to conserve heat. The Y-tracery windows on the south wall were replaced some years ago by PVC frames similar in design and square glazing panels to the original windows. The least sympathetic replacement of frames has been on the three-light east window. Original small windows with diamond-shaped clear glazing, which light the gallery, are located high on the west gable wall on either side of the centrally- placed tower. The south wall is also decorated with distinctive pinnacles surmounting the corners.

The battlemented and very slightly stepped tower of four stages, separated by string courses, has shallow clasping buttresses which are topped with pinnacles matching those on the corners of the hall. On the ground stage of the south wall of the tower there is a door with a gently inward-sloping arch surround and above that, on the second stage, a PVC replacement window, an infilled square opening for the clock on the third stage and a louvred opening on the final belfry stage. There are also four openings on the west wall, an original window with iron frame and square panes of clear glass on the ground stage, openings on the second and third stage similar to those on the south wall but now infilled and a louvred opening on the belfry stage. The louvred opening on the belfry stage is the only one on both north and east walls of the tower.

There is little early information about the original interior arrangements of the church although it is known that box pews were fitted initially. There was a brief report in the Dublin [later Irish] Builder in August 1860 that some changes, by Welland and Gillespie, Ecclesiastical Commissioners' architects, had been made but no details were given. The earliest record of the interior arrangements is found on an undated architectural plan which was probably a precursor of the application for a faculty in May 1867. By that date the box pews had been replaced by bench pews and a vestry room had been added on the north east corner. It would seem also there had been alterations to the area and fittings in the original integral chancel in which there was a comparatively considerable space without seating and the reading desk and pulpit were located on the east wall on either side of the narrow sanctuary. It is probable that those were the changes which had been made in 1860.

Further changes have been made since the 1867 plan was drawn, a number of them probably resulting from the faculty of that year and also reflecting later changes in liturgical practice throughout the Church of Ireland. The pulpit and reading desk were removed from the east wall and the sanctuary, raised on two steps, was increased to the full width of the church. A baptistery with font now occupies the north-west corner of the nave under the panel fronted west gallery which is supported on fluted pillars, one on either side of the centrally-placed aisle. Apart from the low wooden panels in the nave, the walls and ceiling are of plaster and decorated with a moulded cornice.

There are thirteen wall tablets in the church, several of them striking examples of black and white marble memorials typical of the late eighteenth and early nineteenth centuries. Perhaps the most interesting are those depicting naval lives with carvings of fallen masts and sails, anchors, ships' cannon and swords. These memorials are to two brothers, Admiral Sir Josias Rowley and Rear Admiral Samuel Campbell Rowley, who served with distinction in the British Navy for many years, including during the Napoleonic Wars. After long years at sea Sir Josias, who was one of two donors of the gallery seating and the clock soon after the church was consecrated, ended his days at Mount Campbell, Drumsna, which had been the family home of his mother.

Annaduff: St. Ann

ANNESTOWN: ST.ANNE

Annestown, Co. Waterford, is a small coastal village in Dunhill Parish, in the Diocese of Lismore. The settlement may have begun to develop in the early nineteenth century when a garrison was based there during civil unrest in the county and then developed further as sea bathing became more fashionable. The ruined mediaeval parish church, dating from the early Norman occupation and situated one mile inland at Dunhill, was demolished by the Cromwellian Army in 1649. Annestown was chosen as the location when it was decided to build a new parish church in 1819.

According to Rennison, the new church was completed in late 1822 and dedicated to St. Anne on 22 December of that year. There is no record of the dedication or the reason for the choice of name. It may have been the dedication of the mediaeval parish church but no record has been found to confirm that. It is most unlikely to have been named in memory of Queen Anne who died a century earlier but it is possible that the name of the village suggested the dedication.

The simple and neat small edifice with seating for 100 people did not survive for long. After only thirty-three years, it was demolished and replaced on the same site by a slightly larger church which was dedicated to St. John Baptist on 7 October 1856. There is no extant record of the reason for the replacement of the 1822 building or the change of dedication. Based on the present building it is almost certain the earlier church was not liturgically orientated.

Curiously, but erroneously, a church at Annestown, dedicated to St. Anne, appeared in church records during the years 1963-1983 when it was listed together with St. John Baptist, Dunhill, in the Drumcannon Group of churches in the yearly Irish Church Directory. In 1983 the word 'closed' was included after the name of the church and the entry did not appear in subsequent years. Unfortunately this is not an isolated example of poor record-keeping by the Church of Ireland of its built heritage.

Happily some record of the 1822 building has survived among the architectural drawings by James Pain now held at the RCB Library. Pain (c.1799-1877) was the Board of First Fruits architect for some years and then became the Ecclesiastical Commisioners' architect for the area of the former Province of Cashel between 1833 and 1844. The drawings, entitled Annstown [sic] and undated, but probably from some date between 1826 and 1841, contain a south elevation and a plan of walls and interior fittings. These drawings show that it was a typical Board of First Fruits church from the early nineteenth century. It was small with a two-bay rectangular hall and an integrated low two-stage western tower. All openings on the building were pointed. There were windows on both walls of the hall and those on the south wall, and presumably those on the north also, had Y- tracery. On the lower stage of the tower there was a porch door in the west wall and a small window on both north and south walls. Above the porch on the belfry stage of the south wall, and probably on the other three walls, there was a recessed opening with louvres. The tower was surmounted with battlements and had pinnacles on each corner, the only part of this otherwise plain building to have decorative features.

Inside at the liturgical east end of the church there was a narrow integral sanctuary, raised on two steps and surrounded on three sides by seating. There were just eleven bench pews on the north wall and, on the other side of the central aisle, eight on the south wall. The pulpit and reading desk occupied the central area on the south wall. Typically for the period, there was no fixed baptistery area.

Annestown: St. Anne

BELFAST: ST. ANNE'S PARISH CHURCH

By the early 1770s, the old Corporation and parish church, situated in High Street, Belfast, was structurally dangerous and in very poor repair. It was demolished in 1774 and almost forty years later St. George's was built where the former parish church had stood. The site chosen for the new parish church was a short distance away in Donegall Street on land previously occupied [1753-1774] by the second Linen Hall of Belfast.

The new church was completed in 1776 at a cost of £10,000 at the sole expense of the fifth Earl [and first Marquis] of Donegall. There is no extant record of the consecration or dedication of the church. It was originally intended to be dedicated to St. Patrick but was eventually named St. Anne, after the Mother of the Blessed Virgin Mary. This dedication was in memory of the earl's first wife, Anne, daughter of the Duke of Hamilton, who died at Bath in 1780 after a long illness.

The architect was Francis Hiorne of Warwick, who was well known for his Gothic church design. The new parish church was, however, basically a large Georgian preaching box of classical design with a decorated west front and pedimented portico supported on four Corinthian columns and surmounted by a tower. Hiorne was assisted in the building of the church by Roger Mulholland, an important Belfast architect of the late eighteenth century.

The outline of the building on a town plan, circa 1890, shows a rectangular hall with an apse, as wide as the western portico, on the east wall. The east end of the hall may have contained an integral chancel area with the pulpit, reading desk and altar in the linear east-west positions found in many classical churches. This is not certain as the pulpit and reading desk may have been located elsewhere [see below]. There was also an extension on the east wall to the north of the apse, perhaps a vestry, which was not shown on an earlier map, circa 1850.

The church, with three aisles, had accommodation for 990 people exclusively in private pews. There was a western gallery in which the Donegall family had a private pew to which access was gained by a private staircase rising from the vestibule. The Sovereign and Burgesses of Belfast had a large square box pew located in a central position north of the central aisle. It is possible that the pulpit and reading desk may have been located on the other side of the central aisle, opposite the pew reserved for important civic dignitaries attending church. The large Corporation box pew was divided into two in 1870 and the Sovereigns' chair and desk, made of Spanish mahogany carved in Chippendale style, were removed to the vestry.

Arthur Young described the building as 'one of the lightest and most pleasing I have anywhere seen'. Lewis said it consisted 'of a nave and chancel, with a lofty Ionic tower surmounted by a Corinthian cupola covered with copper, forming an interesting and conspicuous object for many miles around'. Benn, in his *History of Belfast*, stated that 'the high and beautiful steeple' was 'rather disproportionate' to the west front. The 1823 engraving, in Benn's book, illustrates the west front with round-headed windows and square panes of clear glass, a low portico and a parapet with balustrades above which rose a four stage tower surmounted by a cupola.

The very low portico, which was not part of the original building, was described by Lewis as being inferior. The *Belfast Newsletter* of 27 July 1832 carried an advertisement inviting proposals for the rebuilding of the portico. It was replaced by a much taller Corinthian structure above which was added, at a later date, a pediment replacing the central balustrade. As a result the clock face, situated on the lowest stage of the tower, was obscured and, subsequently, was moved upwards to the next stage.

A photograph of the church in 1890 provides a view which suggests that the balustrade continued above the north and south walls. There were two storeys of windows on the south wall with tall round-headed windows, similar to those on the west front, situated above shorter segmental-headed lower windows. This together with comments by Sir Thomas Drew confirms that galleries ran around three walls of the nave.

In the final decade of the nineteenth century pressure grew for the construction of a cathedral for the city of Belfast. The decision to go ahead was made in 1896 and the site of St. Anne's Parish Church was selected because of the expense of purchasing a suitably large alternative location close to the city centre. The decision to demolish the parish church appears not to have been widely opposed or lamented although the Irish Builder said it was a sad loss.

In a letter of reply, Sir Thomas Drew, the architect of the new cathedral, said the parish church had a cramped galleried interior without noble design. The walls of rough brick and wooden window sashes had served their time. The only feature of architectural merit was the tower cupola but it was no more than a model in perishable wood of what would be a respectable tower in stone. The portico of much decayed Scrabo sandstone was of little merit. The whole building had sunk so much that the steps on which it had been elevated had disappeared. The only features of merit, he concluded, were the fittings of fine Domingo mahogany which would be carefully preserved.

The tower of the church was removed in 1900 and the skeleton of the new building grew around the old church. The final service was held at the end of 1903 and the church was demolished in early 1904. A few months later the nave of the cathedral was consecrated.

Belfast Parish Church: St. Anne c.1837

BELFAST: ST. ANNE'S CATHEDRAL

A cathedral for the rapidly growing town of Belfast was first proposed by the Dean and Chapter of Connor in 1860. The idea was supported a few years later by a writer [Godkin], somewhat hostile to the established church, who suggested the existing cathedrals at the three 'insignificant' towns of Downpatrick, Dromore and Lisburn should be replaced by one at Belfast. Some thirty years later in 1894, the Bishop of the United Dioceses of Down, Connor and Dromore presented a somewhat illogical scheme, conceived by the Rector of Belfast, to the Diocesan Council for a cathedral at Belfast which would link the existing cathedrals. Civic pride undoubtedly played a major part in overcoming the objections of cost and doubts about the necessity for the building. It would seem that the need to limit costs was an important factor in the selection of the site of the existing parish church for the location of the new cathedral because of the expense of acquiring an alternative close to the city centre.

The architects chosen in 1896 were Thomas Drew and William Henry Lynn, both distinguished former pupils of Lanyon. They were the first of eight architects to work on the construction of the building over a period of eighty years. Lynn subsequently withdrew into the background but retained an advisory role. Drew [1898-1910] initially designed a very traditional early Gothic building with a large square tower over the crossing, a square chancel, a large rose window and ribbed ceiling but he revised his ideas and designed a simplified Romanesque building with some features retained from his original plans. It has been suggested that Lynn was influential in the change of design which would be less expensive and could be built in parts over a longer period of time as money became available.

The foundation stone of the nave was laid in September 1898 and it was consecrated in June 1904. The new design was for a nave of six bays with side aisles, massive piers carrying the clerestory, a tall west gable with a large triple window and provision for a chapel and baptistery opening from the most western bays on the north and south sides respectively. The nave, described as majestic [Williams] and massive, brooding and impressive [Brett], is held to be one of the finest and most successful parts of the cathedral. When Drew died in 1910 much work on the nave remained to be completed.

He was succeeded by Lynn [1910-1915], who designed the baptistery, semi-circular in shape and with a semi-domed roof, to be built on the site indicated in Drew's plans. Lynn died before work commenced on the baptistery. He had worked for some time on modifications to Drew's plans for the crossing as did his successor Peter McGregor Chalmers [1915-1922], who also designed carvings for a capital and corbel. Work on the crossing commenced in 1917 but Chalmers died before it was finished in 1924. Richard Mills Close [1922-1924] supervised the final years of work on the crossing and the start of work on Lynn's baptistery in 1922.

Building of the baptistery continued under the supervision of the new architect, Sir Charles Nicholson [1924-1948], who designed the floor of Portland stone and Irish marble. The mosaic ceiling, symbolising the Creation, is composed of 150,000 pieces of glass each individually placed by hand by two sisters, Gertrude and Margaret Martin. The label stops on the Bath stone string-course were carved by the local sculptor, Rosamund Praeger. The three stained glass windows, with Moses leading the Children of Israel, John the Baptist baptising Jesus in the Jordan and Patrick at Tara, reflect the sacrament of Baptism. The baptistery, which is considered to be one of the finest parts of the cathedral, was consecrated in June 1928.

Nicholson was also working at this time on completing the decoration of Drew's nave. He designed both the paving using different colours of Irish marble [completed 1929] and carvings for the remaining nine unfinished capitals and corbels on the massive piers. Between 1925 and 1937, Morris Harding carved eight of the capitals and corbels with the others being carved by Rosamund Praeger. Harding, an Englishman, settled in Belfast and was later President of the Royal Society of Ulster Architects.

Prior to the appointment of Nicholson, the Cathedral Board had decided to replace the temporary west front on which the brickwork had become rather shabby. The design of the new front, to be a memorial to those who had died in World War I, was Nicholson's first major task. He based the design on Drew's plans, retaining the triple windows but replacing the deeply recessed gable portals with three arched porches and added arcading and carved label stops on the upper part of the gable and capstones on the turrets. The sculptures on the tympanum were by Esmond Burton, an English sculptor who had worked on major war memorials in England. Brett considered the Nicholson West Front to be a remarkable anthology of architectural styles but found the carvings on the tympanum unimpressive. The foundation stone of the west front was laid in June 1925 and dedicated two years later. Nicholson also designed the bronze gates for the portals which were added in 1929.

Harding's sense of fun can be seen in his carvings of the four label stops high on the west gable, which represent industry, strife, love and greed, the four ruling passions of life. His carvings, the four aces, depict industry by a man digging with a spade, strife by two men fighting with clubs, love by a couple holding hands while standing on a heart and greed by a miser clutching his money while perched on a diamond.

The Chapel of the Holy Spirit, on which work commenced in 1930, was the final part of the cathedral to be added before the Great Depression of the 1930s and then World War II brought a halt to further building. Rectangular with a dome-shaped ceiling and on Drew's intended site, it was consecrated in 1932 to commemorate the 1500th anniversary of St. Patrick coming to Ireland. The mosaics on the entrance arches, depicting the patron saint arriving on a boat, and of the Four Seraphims on the ceiling, were also the work of Gertrude and Margaret Martin. These mosaics together with those in Baptistery and above the West Door represent a total of seven years work by the two sisters, who had previously worked on Westminster Cathedral.

The cathedral miraculously escaped serious damage during the heavy bombing of Belfast by German aircraft in 1941 when adjacent buildings were destroyed. Work to complete the building commenced again in 1947 with the design of the eastern apse and ambulatory by Nicholson, then aged 79, and his partner and successor, Thomas H. Rushton [1948-1963]. Building work started in 1955 and was completed in 1959. The stained glass window now on the east wall of the apse had been installed first in the old parish church of St. Anne's in 1887. Rushton's later proposal for an eastern chapel beyond the apse and a great offset eastern tower and chapter house was abandoned.

Rushton's successor, John McGeagh [1963-1979], designed the south and north transepts in 1964 and 1969, respectively. Work commenced on them in 1969 and the south transept, containing the rather uninspiring Chapel of Unity and the Organ, was completed in 1974. Work stopped on the north transept in the same year owing to financial difficulties and for some years the girders of the unfinished transept were visible. It was eventually finished to McGeagh's design by his successor, Robert McKinstry [1979-1986] and dedicated in 1981. The internal part of this transept, containing a regimental chapel, is rather shallow owing to the large deep Celtic Cross on the external gable which one writer considered to be somewhat out of place in a Romanesque building [Galloway].

With the dedication of that transept, the cathedral was now considered to be complete. Brett, who in 1967 had considered the unfinished building to be an unsatisfactory edifice with a disconcerting confusion of styles and disparate parts, later stated the successive architects had come close to solving the insoluble. Galloway described the completed building as being 'broad, spacious, massive and dignified' and 'a great tribute to the enormous energy and enthusiasm of those who conceived it'. He believed however that it was incomplete without a tower, preferably, or a spire to crown it. Plans for a central tower [Drew], offset eastern tower [Rushton]], spire [McGeagh] and fleche [McKinstry] were all abandoned.

The landscaping, in 1998, of the muddy, potholed car park area around the cathedral and the changes made in 2003 to the west front to provide disabled access contributed much to enhance the cathedral. In 2006, the view that the cathedral was incomplete without a tower or spire surmounting the crossing finally prevailed. Opinion however is divided as to whether the slim stainless steel spire erected in early 2007 is in harmony and balance with the architectural style and size of the cathedral or has enhanced it.

Although the cathedral is dedicated to St. Anne there is little in the fabric to reflect this. One of eighteen figures, four of them female, carved high on the tympanum represents St Anne but strangely there is no stained glass window depicting the saint. The Calendar of the Church of Ireland has never included St. Anne amongst the saints for whom liturgical provision is made and there is no evidence to suggest that her feast day on 26 July was ever kept at Belfast Cathedral as the patronal festival. Rather curiously, and somewhat in keeping with pre-Reformation tradition, there is a special service each year to mark the anniversary of the consecration of the nave.

Belfast Cathedral: St. Anne

BLENNERVILLE: ST. ANNA

The parish of Blennerville, sometimes called by its ecclesiastical name of Annagh [Annagh – a marshy place] or St. Anna, is located close to Tralee, Co. Kerry, in the Diocese of Ardfert. The earliest extant record of the parish, dated 1408, notes the name of rector, Maurice Ykahill [O'Cahill]. It is possible that the dedication of the church to St. Anna took place in mediaeval times. Tralee town was founded by Anglo-Normans in the early thirteenth century and settlers during the following two centuries may have brought the cult of devotion to St. Anne with them from England. The Blennerhassett family was granted land in Co. Kerry, circa 1589, by Queen Elizabeth I. Sir Rowland Blennerhassett, 1st Baronet, settled at Cathair Ui Mhorain, near Tralee, around 1762 and renamed it Blennerville.

By 1756 the mediaeval church in the parish was stated to have become ruinous [Smith]. Later records suggest it had a bell, dated 1744. There was no parish church in existence in 1817 according to the ecclesiastical register of that year [Erck] in which the parish was listed as part of the Ballynaheglish Union. The Ecclesiastical Commissioners Report, 1835, listed a new church which had been built 'at Blennerville in the parish of St. Anna' in 1818. The church building was described in 1837 [Lewis] as being a neat modern structure with a square tower while the Parliamentary Gazetteer stated, in 1844, that it was capable of seating 250 and had a regular attendance of 180 on Sundays.

There are architectural drawings of the church, undated but probably prior to 1844, by James Pain, the Board of First Fruits architect for some years and then Ecclesiastical Commisioners' architect for the former Province of Cashel 1833-1844. The drawings, which contain plans and a south elevation, show the church to be a three-bay rectangular hall with a western tower, typical of Board of First Fruit designs of the period.

There are several distinctive features depicted on the drawings. A small vestry extending from the middle bay on the north side provided access to the north wall pulpit below which there was a reading desk and font. A transept extending from the middle bay on the south wall was of sufficient length to make the church into a T-shape. There was an integral chancel within the hall at the east end and a gallery above the west end to which access was gained by a staircase in the tower. The only opening on the lower stage of the tower was a door on the north wall. A south elevation depicts a pointed opening with louvres in a recess on the upper stage, pointed windows with lattice glazing in the nave and a transept which was not built. The tower was surmounted by a battlement with finials at the corners from which thin pinnacles rose.

The plan of the building and arrangement of fittings with all box and single pews facing the centrally placed pulpit, emphasising the importance of preaching, is reminiscent of T-shaped Presbyterian and a few Church of Ireland churches of the eighteenth century. As often with nineteenth century church plans it would seem, however, that the plans depicted a composition of the original building together with Pain's proposals for enlargement of the church.

Architectural drawings of this type were usually precursors of proposed alterations to the structure and or reordering of the interior fittings of the church but the vestry minutes of the period make no reference to any such changes. Most of the minutes are concerned with the appointment of churchwardens and the costs of i] arrangements for foundlings and deserted children, ii] paupers' coffins, iii] the purchase of turf which heated the building from Christmas to Easter and iv] the recurring repairs to the roof and steeple.

A local history of Blennerville published in 1989 provides evidence that the proposed extensions were not built. It contains two illustrations with a rather small St. Anna's Church in the distance. Unfortunately, despite a major effort, the originals of those photographs or indeed any other illustrations of the church were not found. Although the church building is distant in the photographs they show clearly that the small vestry on the middle bay of the north side and the much larger south transept had not been built. The 1989 publication also contains details of a large marble wall monument in the church with 'highly artistic' carvings of symbols of battle in memory of a 19 year old soldier, originally from the parish, who died on active service in India in 1857.

By 1869 the number of parishioners in the three parishes of the union had fallen to 191 and thirteen years later in 1882 the church, presumably closed by then, was not listed in the Irish Church Directory of that year. It remained for quite some time as a roofless ruin until it was demolished around 50 years later. In a 1967 Ardfert Diocesan Magazine, some old residents of Blennerville recalled the village with many Church of Ireland people and the lovely church with its steeple, bell and churchyard. The bell, which had been in the ruined mediaeval church, was installed in the 1818 building. On demolition of the church, circa 1935, the bell would seem to have been taken to St. Michael and All Angels, Dromod [Waterville, Diocese of Ardfert] where it was found in the churchyard in 1951 [Dukes].

The ruined church and the churchyard were handed over to Tralee Urban District Council in 1981 with the condition that the churchyard would be restored and maintained in keeping with its former use. The ruin was removed and the site became a park named after Robert Emmett, the nineteenth century Irish Patriot. The connection of the Emmett family with the area dates back to 1791 when Robert's cousin owned land in the parish.

The patriot's burial place has long been a subject of interest and investigation. There has always been a tradition that, after his execution at Dublin, Emmett's body, without the head, was buried in St. Anna's Churchyard. Despite much research by the Emmett Society no conclusive evidence has been found to support the tradition. The bicentenary commemoration of his execution was held at the Robert Emmett Park on 20 July 2003.

Blennerville: St. Anna

CAPPOQUIN: ST. ANNE

St. Anne's, Cappoquin, Co. Waterford, in the Diocese of Lismore, is situated on the main street of the small town in the beautiful wooded countryside of the lower Blackwater Valley.

In 1814 the Dean and Chapter of Lismore resolved that the district of Cappoquin [Ceapach Choinn – Conn's tillage plots] would become a perpetual curacy at such a time as a church should be built there. A curate was appointed in 1819 and in October of the following year a small church was consecrated and dedicated to St. Anne. There is no extant record of the reason for the dedication but it may have been in memory of Bishop Stock's mother.

James Pain's architectural plans of the building in 1835 show it to be a typical simple plain church of that period with a three-bay rectangular hall, pointed Y-tracery windows, and integrated west tower. At the east end of the hall, the integral chancel occupied a raised central position on the east wall with a bow shaped altar rail around the sanctuary which was flanked by the pulpit and reading desk. Two large box pews occupied the east end of the nave on either side of the centrally-placed aisle with smaller box pews on the remainder of the north wall and bench pews on the south.

The 1835 plans were drawn apparently as the first step in the addition of a vestry which was to be situated on the north-east corner of the hall but it was not built. The drawings include an elevation of the church showing a slender octagonal broached spire. Lewis [1837] described the church as a neat edifice with a spire and the Parliamentary Gazetteer of 1844 stated that 'a church in the town lifts a very pretty spire from among the cluster of cabins'. There is no record of the removal of the spire.

There were major changes to the church in 1869 when a vestry and a chancel extension were built. The vestry, first considered over thirty years earlier, was now built to the south of, but separated from, the chancel wall. The area of the new chancel was raised on three steps and the altar rail was positioned at the chancel arch thus effectively using the extension as a large sanctuary. It is probable that the beautifully carved panelling and reredos, with a central niche and canopy, were installed in the sanctuary at the same time. Stained glass depicting the four Gospel writers was installed in the traceried three-light east window in 1877.

A reordering of the nave was also carried out. The pulpit remained in the original place and the two large box pews were removed to provide space for a chancel area containing the lectern and reading desk. The lower walls of the nave were panelled and the floors of the chancel, sanctuary and aisle were tiled. It may have been at this time, or possibly somewhat earlier, that the north-west corner of the nave was altered to provide a baptistery with a fixed font. Prior to this baptisms took place in the chancel area using a portable font. The original pulpit was replaced in 1897 by a stone and marble one of typical late Victorian style.

The original Y-tracery and square panes of glass in the narrow pointed nave windows have been replaced, at date unknown, with opaque slightly coloured panes of different shapes. The nave walls above the very plain panelling are plastered and overhead the roof and wooden panelling of the ceiling are carried by braced arch trusses resting on corbels.

On the exterior of the church, the random rubble walls are rendered in a rather dull grey colour. The only decorative features on the otherwise plain exterior are found on the integrated tower on which the three stages are marked by string-courses. The church doorway on the west wall of the ground stage has a pointed recessed arch and at the upper belfry stage there are recessed Y-tracery louvres above which the tower is surmounted by a simple battlemented parapet with coping stones. The tower contains a small bell with an inscription naming the maker and the year of installation, 'Woods and Barnes, Miller Street, Cork, 1819'.

Cappoquin: St. Anne

CARLOW: ST. ANNE

In 1841, a committee of Tipperary Conservatives was formed to raise a testimonial fund for a presentation to Colonel Henry Bruen of Oak Park, Carlow, who had won a rather unexpected victory by just nine votes over John O'Connell, son of Daniel, in the election for the Borough of Carlow. A year later £2000 had been raised and the committee proposed to present him with a gold watch. Colonel Bruen declined the offer of a personal gift and suggested that the money should be used for something dear to his heart, the erection of a free church in Carlow which 'had long been needed for the increasing number of parishioners'. The committee agreed to this request and the Colonel donated a site on his estate and undertook financial responsibility for the erection and fitting of the church which he knew would be greatly in excess of the amount existing in the testimonial fund.

The architect chosen by the Colonel was John MacDuff Derick, a native of Sligo, who had designed churches in England and Ireland in the 1830s and 1840s. The Colonel, who was widely travelled and deeply interested in architecture, may have met the architect when attending Parliament in London. Derick was a founder member of the Oxford Society for Promoting the Study of Gothic Architecture, established in 1839, and a friend of Pugin, the foremost British Victorian Gothic architect. Derick's early churches, however, were of classical design but his later work, including St. Anne's Carlow, was mainly in Gothic style.

The construction of the building was delayed and the foundation stone was not laid until 21 May 1852. Colonel Bruen died six months later and his son, Henry, assumed financial responsibility for the church. It was completed in 1858 but there is no record of the date of consecration. The Rural Dean's Visitation Report of 1862 records that it was being used for worship but had not yet been consecrated. There is also no record of the reason for the dedication to St. Anne but it seems most likely that it was named in memory of Colonel Bruen's wife, Anne Wandesforde nee Kavanagh, who had died in 1850.

Henry endowed the church, and with his right of nomination, appointed the perpetual curate of the adjoining parish of Painestown to the same postion at St. Anne's. The link with Painestown was to remain throughout the comparatively short life of the church even when they both became part of the Carlow Union.

The Rural Dean's Visitation Reports from the early twentieth century record a slow decline in the numbers attending the customary service on Sunday afternoons. The further decline in attendance after Partition in 1921 resulted in closure in 1923 or 1924. Although it was sold in 1925 the church continued to be listed in the yearly Church of Ireland Directory as Painestown, St. Anne, until 1944 in which year it was stated to be 'closed or demolished'.

The building was purchased in 1925 by the Very Reverend James Bolger, PP., as a replacement for a small Catholic church in Graiguecullen. St. Anne's was then dismantled stone by stone and transported the short distance to Graiguecullen, a small village in Co. Laois across the River Barrow from Carlow town. The stones were used to build a new church, without the spire, which was consecrated and dedicated to St. Clare in 1928. The stones of the spire were stored in the chapel yard for later construction but they disappeared during renovations in the 1960s.

A few sources appear to suggest that, apart from the spire, the new church was a rebuild of St. Anne's. Unfortunately there is no extant ground plan of St. Anne's to compare it with St. Clare's but it is very obvious, however, from the photograph of St. Anne's c.1924, that while there are some similarities there are fundamental and significant differences between the two churches.

The design of St. Clare's retained the basic cruciform ground plan, the stone mullioned windows, the roof trusses and many of the external decorative features such as the hood mouldings, carved label stops and gargoyles. The major changes in design were the introduction of side aisles and chapels on either side of the nave and chancel, respectively, and a short clerestory with quatrefoil windows and relocation of the central tower to the [liturgical] north west corner and the south facing porch to the [liturgical] west entrance.

St. Anne's, built of Wicklow granite of three different colours, was cruciform in plan with a four-bay nave, two-bay transepts and chancel. There were large windows of five lights on the east gable and of four lights on the other gables, all with elaborate tracery and hood mouldings rising from richly carved corbels. On the lower walls, the windows were of two lights and in common with other windows had dressed stone mullions and surrounds and were decorated with hood mouldings and carved label stops. Yorkshire stone was used in the window tracery and mullions and also the gargoyle figures on the eaves and at the base of the broached spire. Corners and walls were ornamented with stepped diagonal and inter bay buttresses respectively.

The large yet graceful tower, surmounted by a tall and elegant broached octagonal spire, rose dramatically above the crossing and dominated the church. There were two double-light traceried belfry windows on each face, with decorative features matching those on the other window openings of the church, and stepped angular buttress-like features at each corner of the tower. The spire was decorated with eight hooded lucarnes, of which four had very narrow twin traceried lancets and four were smaller and blind, all with pinnacles on the gables. The spire was topped by a cross and there were cross shaped finials on the four gable apexes. Access to the tower was gained, from within the church and perhaps also by an external door, by an apsidal turret on which there was a pyramidal cap topped with a crocketed pinnacle.

St. Anne's Church, Carlow, before it was demolished.

Carlow: St. Anne

Perhaps the most obvious features in a photograph of the interior, taken at some date between closure and demolition, are the massive deeply splayed and moulded piers at the crossing and the arches which supported the weight of the tower and spire. A door carved in the south east pier was the internal entrance to the tower staircase. The interior was less decorated than the exterior of the building although there were hood mouldings with carved label stops on the window arches. The floor was of encaustic tiles and, above, the high pitched roof was of diagonally sheeted open timber work. The strong influence of Tractarianism, with its greater emphasis on sacramental worship, on the design of the church is reflected in the raised chancel, sanctuary steps and provision for a raised altar. The altar and pulpit had been removed when the photograph was taken but the carved octagonal font in the south west corner remained.

At some date prior to the consecration of the church, Father McCabe, a Roman Catholic Parish Priest in Dublin, later Archbishop of Dublin (1879-1885) and Cardinal from 1882, made a visit to the church. He was one of the many who considered it to be one of the finest examples of Gothic Revival architecture to be built in Ireland. According to *The Builder* of 28 August 1858 the building cost £12000.

CASTLEMARTYR: ST. ANNE

St. Anne's, Castlemartyr, in the Diocese of Cloyne, is situated, at the upper end of a nineteenth century lime walk, on a low hill above the main street of the small town in East Cork. The church, described as handsome in 1824 [Pigot], replaced the old parish church of Ballyoughtera, built 1549, which was destroyed in the 1641 Rebellion.

By an Act of Parliament, 9 Anne c.12, 1710, the former parishes of Ballyoughtera, Mogeely and Caherultan were united to form a new parish to be called Castlemartyr. The new parish church, which was to be situated at the borough of that name on ground given by Henry Boyle, Speaker of Irish House of Commons and later Earl of Shannon, was not built until 1731. There is no extant record of the dedication of the either the 1549 or 1731 church although it would seem most likely that the new church was named in memory of Queen Anne as a result of the 1710 Act.

The early Vestry Minutes provide little information about the fabric of the building or the fittings apart from costs of repairs. In 1769 the minutes recorded much concern about the large number of 'strolling vagabonds and beggars infesting the parish' who mixed with the poor and indigent inhabitants 'thus obstructing the works of charity'. The Earl of Shannon gave fifty brass badges to be worn by the parish poor and built almshouses. The Rural Deanery Visitation Reports of the 1790s recorded that the church roof and slating were in very poor repair causing considerable dampness on the walls. A major storm in 1798 caused serious breaches in the roof and walls. Further major repairs, costing £225, were necessary in 1832 but no details were recorded in the minutes.

An undated ground plan, drawn by James Pain at some date between 1825 and 1841, provides information about the probable original ordering of the fittings of the church. The plan of the building and the fittings recorded are similar to those of other churches built in the classical style of the early eighteenth century. It shows a rectangular hall of five bays, with the sanctuary in a semicircular east end apse squared off on the exterior wall and an integrated tower at the west. The pulpit and reading desk were situated at the only window on the middle of the north nave wall and no baptistery was marked. The seating accommodation was of box pews of variable size on either side of the centrally-placed aisle. The largest box pew, situated at the north east corner of the nave, was the family pew of the Earls of Shannon. Such plans, as that drawn by Pain, were usually the first stage in the reordering of internal fittings or alterations to the fabric but there is no reference in the Vestry Minutes of the period to any such work being undertaken.

The present interior of the church shows many changes from the undated ground plan. These changes may have taken place during the mid 1860s, a period when the interiors of a number of early Georgian churches in Ireland were reordered. Alternatively the changes may have been part of the improvements and enlargements made in the late 1860s to provide accommodation for the parishioners of Ightermurragh Parish Church which closed in 1870.

The panel-fronted shallow gallery at the west end, which was not marked on the ground plan, was almost certainly added to provide extra seating for those new parishioners. It is supported on three simple columns, one on either side of the centrally-positioned aisle and one rising from a window sill on the south wall, and three corbel stones inserted on the west and north walls. Access to the gallery is gained from narrow twin staircases rising from the porch.

The pulpit and reading desk were removed from the north wall to a new chancel area situated at the east end of the nave. The tall wooden wall panelling with beautifully carved pediment and fluted pilasters, formerly part of the Earls of Shannon's family pew, remains in situ as part of the chancel. The other box pews were replaced by typical Victorian bench pews apart from the south west corner where the baptistery is situated. The font of carved limestone has no date or inscription but it is most probably Victorian.

All openings on the building are round-headed. Those in the nave windows, which are of two lights, have original wooden framework with square panes of clear glass. The Victorian style stained glass of the east window depicting the Ascension of Jesus, which was installed as a war memorial in 1922, is, rather unfortunately, out of keeping with the remainder of the glazing and the classical Georgian church.

The original flagged stone floor is currently covered by carpet which provides warmth but detracts from the classical church. The walls of the nave and apse are plastered and have an elaborate cornice with a cable decorative motif. There is an interesting wall memorial in late eighteenth century style, perhaps the only such work by a local master stone mason named Broad. Another notable feature of the interior is the plastered single vault ceiling without the supports found in other similar churches.

On the exterior of the building, the walls appear, from the places where the rendering has fallen off, to be of uncoursed rubble. There is a marked difference in the decorative features on the north and south facing sides of the church. The north wall, which contains only one window and on which there is a low vestry at the northwest corner, is plain without any form of decoration. The south side of the church, facing the path up through the lime walk, has a dressed stone cornice, a wide strip of dressed stone, incorporating hood mouldings for the five windows, on the walls of the nave and apse and quoins at the corners of the nave.

The building is dominated to some extent by the slightly stepped wide tower of three stages divided by thin string courses. The west facing doorway with fanlight and Gibbsian surround is the only opening on the lowest stage. There are deeply recessed louvres on three faces of the belfry stage which contains a bell made in Dublin, or possibly by Graham, Founders, Waterford, but without date or inscription. Above that on the shorter top stage there are circular openings also with louvres on each face. The tower is surmounted by low battlements with coping stones.

This is indeed, as Pigot described it in 1824, a handsome building, one of those modest and largely unknown architectural treasures of the church. A quarter of a century away from its tercentenary, it is in need of restoration. It must be hoped that it will take place in the not too distant future.

Castlemartyr: St. Anne

SHANDON: ST. ANNE

St. Anne's, Shandon, is situated in the city and Diocese of Cork, on high ground to the north of the River Lee from where its tall distinctive tower is visible over a wide area. There has been a church on the site from at least 1199, some twenty years after the Normans came to Cork but there may have been an earlier church as Shandon [Sean Dun – the old fort] was possibly the royal residence of the McCarthy Kings of Desmond.

The mediaeval church, dedicated to St. Mary, was close to Shandon Castle. The church was severely damaged in 1690 during an attack on the castle by the beseiging Williamite army. A new parish church, with the same dedication, was built in 1696 closer to the river at Lower Shandon and away from what was perceived as dangerous proximity to the castle. This church was demolished in 1879.

As the Shandon area began to grow in economic importance in the early eighteenth century, a chapel of ease to St. Marys', was built on the site of the old mediaeval church. This chapel, erected by public subscription, was completed in 1722 and dedicated to St. Anne. Almost twenty years later it was suggested [Smith] that the dedication was chosen because St. Anne was the mother of the Blessed Virgin Mary to whom the parish church was dedicated. It seems more likely that it was given the name in memory of Queen Anne, who died in 1714. During her reign, she had shown interest in the Church of Ireland by supporting legislation making it easier to build new churches and by remitting First Fruits from the Crown to the Church.

The design and building of St. Anne's has been ascribed traditionally to John Coltsman, a master stonemason, who may have been responsible for the design of other structures in Cork in the early eighteenth century although little else is know about him. His design of a Georgian preaching box, basilican in style and rectangular in plan with an almost semi-circular east end apse, squared-off on the exterior, and a tower at the west end, was characteristic of several single cell provincial or rural churches of that time according to Craig. It was one of several churches built during the energetic and reforming episcopacy of Peter Brown [1709-1735].

Rather uniquely, the building was constructed of two strongly contrasting colours of stone. The south and west faces of the original tower and all of the later tower extension are of very pale grey ashlar limestone while the remainder of the building is of dark red ashlar sandstone apart from window dressings, the cornice under the eaves and quoins which are of limestone. Tradition has it that the building materials used came from the ruins of Shandon Castle and a local Franciscan Abbey but the quality of the stonework after almost three centuries of erosion suggests that they may have been quarried at the time of building.

The original tower, comparatively massive yet graceful, had three stepped stages topped with a low slightly battlemented parapet. The doorway, which faces west along Church Street, is an aedicule being flanked by fluted pilasters and surmounted by a pediment.   Work on the three-stage addition to the tower began in 1749. At the corners of the upper stage of the original tower and on the first two additional stages there are pineapple-shaped sculptures which were a common feature in eighteenth century ecclesiastical architecture in Cork. The final stage is surmounted by a golden cupola to which was added later the famous gilded weathervane in the shape of a salmon, symbolising the important fisheries nearby on the River Lee.

Eight bells, of which the tenor weighs 26 cwt, were cast by Rudhall at Gloucester and first rung in 1752. Prior to 1906 the bells were hung for full circle ringing but in that year they were placed in a fixed, or 'dead', position and converted to ringing as a chime to reduce the effects of vibration on the tower structure. The 'Bells of Shandon' were made famous by the poem of that name by Francis Sylvester O'Mahony, alias Fr. Prout, whose remains lie in the churchyard. The first bell at St. Anne's, also cast by Rudhall, had been installed in 1745. When the new bells arrived it was removed and installed at the parish church, St. Mary's, Lower Shandon, in 1752. It was removed when that church was demolished in 1879 and is now at St. Mary's, Sundays Wells.

In 1843 the Cork Corporation decided to place a clock on the widely visible tower so that the ordinary people of Cork would be able to know the time. John Mangan, a Cork architect and clockmaker, won the public competition and the clock was installed in 1847. The hours and quarters are struck on the tower bells. The clock is still in public ownership and maintained by the Corporation. For nearly one hundred and forty years until repaired in 1986, the minute hands on the north and south faces lagged behind the others between the half and full hour thus giving rise to a local name for the clock, 'the four-faced liar'.

The 1866 plan of the original church interior depicts a typical classical church of the early eighteenth century with four bays, box pews and galleries around three sides of the nave. The pulpit and reading desk stood at the east end of the nave in front of the altar in the sanctuary and the font was situated at the north-east corner of the nave. The plan also depicts a transept-like extension placed mid-way on the north wall which contained a vestry and an area with a small organ and choir seating. In the reordering which took place in that year, the north and south wall galleries were removed, the box pews were replaced and the pulpit and reading desk were moved from their central position to the north-east and south-east corners of the nave.

Considerable changes were also made during the incumbency of W.J. Galway, 1882-1897. A new pulpit and reading desk of bath stone and marble, typical of that late Victorian era, replaced the former fittings. A new panelled wooden ceiling in the nave, carried by simple roof trusses resting on the walls, concealed the original single vault plaster ceiling. An elaborate dentilled cornice may have been added to the plaster walls in the nave at the same time. In the apse, the vaulted ceiling was also concealed by wooden panelling, a new reredos was installed and, alas, three original clear glass windows were replaced by Victorian stained glass. A further small stained glass window, oval in shape, by Hubert McGoldrick of An Tur Gloine, was installed in the nave in 1939.

Fortunately two ancient fittings remain. A font, of square design on an octagonal shaft, presented to St. Mary's in 1629, was not damaged in the attack on the castle in 1690 which led to the demolition of the church. It was given, at a later but unrecorded date, to St. Anne's. The rare early eighteenth century wooden communion rail, with an elliptical central section and carved balusters, installed in 1722, has also survived the passage of time.

The building is undergoing gradual restoration. During work on the interior of the church, most of the pews installed in 1866 were replaced by chairs, the wooden panelled front on the gallery was painted white and the walls were painted in a lighter colour which cumulatively have helped to brighten the previously rather dark building.

Not everyone, however, has considered it to be a fine church. Smith, in 1774, described it as 'a very neat plain church'. A former Chancellor of the Diocese of Cork [Webster] stated, in 1909, that 'the building had nothing to recommend it as a specimen of architecture except be it in its eccentricities of design and execution'. Tourists, however, come in large numbers to see the church, attracted by its place in the history of Cork, the unique tower, the famous Shandon Bells and the two ancient fittings.

Cork, Shandon: St. Anne

DRUMGLASS: ST. ANNE

St. Anne's, Drumglass, is situated in the town of Dungannon, Co. Tyrone, in the Diocese of Armagh. The first reference to the parish of Drumglass [Druim Glas – the green ridge] is found in the Papal Taxation of the early thirteenth century and the first recorded rector, William M'Kthmayll, was appointed in 1378. The post-Reformation church was destroyed during the Nine Years War, 1594-1603. A new parish church, on the same site, was built by Sir Arthur Chichester in fulfilment of one of the conditions required of him by the grant of land he received from King James at the Ulster Plantation. The Pynnar Survey of 1618 reported that the unfinished church was 'large ...... with a steeple, all of lime and sandstone and now ready to be covered' [roofed with shingles]. Sir Arthur died without issue and his estate passed to his brother Edward, whose descendant built St. Anne's Parish Church, Belfast.

This church, described in 1622 as 'in length 60 foot ... in breadth within walls 25 foot ..... steeple is twentie foot square and fortie foot high the batlement', was destroyed and the rector murdered during the 1641 Rebellion. It was restored in part in 1656, further restored in 1672 and rebuilt in 1692 after the Williamite Wars. Work continued on the church and the steeple was increased in height in 1695. The first record of the dedication to St. Anne is found in the Vestry Minute Book which states that a ' meeting was held in the Parish Church of St. Anne, Drumglass, on Easter Monday, 1st April, 1700'.

The shingle roof was replaced by slates in 1763. Almost twenty years later the church was in poor repair but was used for the first Volunteer Convention in 1782. A colour print, from a later date, in the vestry depicts some of the 242 Volunteers marching to a gaily decorated church. By 1785 the fabric had deteriorated further into a ruinous condition and some years later services were being held in the Presbyterian Meeting House.

Repaired, and perhaps rebuilt to some extent, in 1795, at a cost of £600 and reopened for worship the following year, the church was described in the 1798 Diocesan Report as being exceedingly handsome with a large gallery. Aisles [illustrations suggest transepts] were added in 1812, using a grant of £800 from the Board of First Fruits, to accommodate the growing population of the parish. By 1860 the church was yet again too small for the congregation and it was decided to build a new church.

The old building was taken down in 1867 but fortunately pictorial evidence of it has survived on the colour print and a nineteenth century photograph. These illustrations depict a Planter Gothic church of reversed orientation with the liturgical west front facing eastwards down Church Street. The west gable walls had battlemented parapets with finials at the corners and, on either side of the centrally placed tower, tall windows with Y-tracery on the lower wall and, above them, shorter windows providing light for the gallery. The high slightly stepped tower of three stages, with Y-tracery belfry louvres on the upper stage and large clock on the middle stage, was topped with finials and surmounted by an octagonal spire. A large bell, cast by C & G Mears of London and bearing an inscription dated 1846, was installed in the tower in the following year.

The Minutes of the Select Vestry contain undated nineteenth century plans of the layout of ground floor and gallery. These plans show that the 'aisles' added in 1812 were transepts positioned at the west end of the church thus making it T-shaped. The sanctuary was narrow and rectangular in shape with a semicircular area extending towards the nave. The gallery, which contained an organ loft and choir area at the west end, was accessed by twin staircases rising from the vestibule. It was a large gallery running along each wall of the nave and transepts and had obviously been extended in 1812.

Work on the new church commenced on the same site in 1867 and, retaining the dedication to St. Anne, it was consecrated on 24 September, 1869. Unimpeded by the financial problems which were to affect the Church of Ireland after the forthcoming disestablishment, the cost was £8500 of which half was provided by a grant from the Ecclesiastical Commissioners. The architect was William Joseph Barre of Belfast, one of the most vigorous High Victorian architects in Ulster [Rowan]. Drumglass Church is held to be his masterpiece but sadly he did not live to see it completed as he died in 1867 when the work was in its early stages. It is believed that his design for Drumglass was an adaptation of his unsuccessful entry for the competition to design St. Finbarre's Cathedral, Cork.

The 1869 church is a large building of cathedral-like dimensions, cruciform in shape, very richly decorated in Gothic details, and, like its predecessor, liturgically reversed in orientation because of the shape of the site. It has a four-bay nave, wide two-bay transepts and one-bay chancel with a shallow sanctuary. On the [liturgical] south side there is an asymmetrical lean-to aisle and a gabled porch on the transept and a double gabled porch on the north transept. The massive offset three-stage tower, surmounted by pinnacles and a broached spire with lucarnes, and the impressive [liturgical] west front, with its tall gable and deeply recessed large rose window, dominate Church Street and rise well above the surrounding buildings. The bell from the old church was installed in the new tower along with two other smaller bells cast by J.C.Wilson of Glasgow, one of which was recast in 1952.

The exterior of the building was never fully completed to the architect's plans. Barre had designed three Celtic Crosses to be placed on the apexes of the west and transept gables. The builder, when preparing to erect them, was approached by some men from Killyman who considered it was 'romish' to have a cross on the church. The vestry would seem to have yielded to the intimidation because none were erected. One source suggests the men removed the crosses and buried them. Another suggests that two of the crosses were preserved by Lord Ranfurly in his estate grounds. Two have been recovered, one being unearthed when the new Parish Hall was being built and the other from the grounds of the Manor Court of the former estate. One of them now stands in the Garden of Remembrance and it is planned to erect the other in the new garden also in the church grounds.

The first impression on entering by the south [liturgical] transept door is, in comparison with the exterior, a little disappointing and the absence of a matching north aisle and lack of colour on the unusually tall opaque windows make the north wall of the nave somewhat dull yet the church is richly adorned and there are many attractive features. It is spacious with two large transepts and has high moulded chancel and transept arches, a pine fronted west gallery and large multi-light windows on the transept and east gables. The high braced trusses of the steeply raked roof are supported on polished stone colonettes rising from corbels at clerestory level. New sanctuary tiling, a carved reredos, and oak choir stalls were installed in the chancel in 1910 and further panelling was added in 1933.

Much of the stained glass is of typical Victorian design in rather dark colours but the large seven-light transept gable windows are glazed in rich bright colours. The gable window in the [liturgical] south transept, which replaced one destroyed by bomb blast, depicts children of all races gathering round the tree of knowledge and church organisations relating to childhood. The original rose window, also destroyed by bomb blast, has been replaced by attractive modern glass. There is a baptistery window by A.E. Child of An Tur Gloine, 1938, and the World War II Memorial window in the south transept, 1951, is by the famous studio of James Powell of London. A two-light window in the [liturgical] south aisle depicts St. Anne, in the traditional pose of instructing the Blessed Virgin Mary during childhood, and Anna, the prophetess in the Temple at the Presentation of Christ.

There are a large number of memorials, in the form of wall tablets, a 1696 tombstone now in the north porch, stained glass windows including the large seven-light east window and fittings such as the octagonal marble font of 1876, to the Earls of Ranfurly, and members of their families, who were generous benefactors of the church. On the departure of his family from Dungannon in 1927, Lord Ranfurly presented to the church five copper collecting boxes which had been used in the old parish church.

Drumglass: St. Anne- demolished 1867

Drumglass: St. Anne

DUBLIN, DAWSON ST: ST. ANN

As the urban area of early eighteenth century Dublin expanded slowly southwards, the parish of St. Anne was created out of three adjoining parishes by Act of Parliament, 6 Anne c 21, of 30 October 1707, to cater for the growing population. Reflecting its early surroundings, it was at least once referred to as 'St. Anne in the Cornfields'. The site originally chosen for the church was on the west side of what is now Dawson Street but it may have been changed to the other side to allow the west doors of the liturgically orientated church to open on to the street. It seems likely that the dedication may have been chosen as much in honour of Queen Anne, who was generous towards the Church of Ireland, as of the mother of the Blessed Virgin Mary. Rather strangely the spelling of the parish name was changed, at an early stage, to St. Ann although it was called St. Anne in the original Act of Parliament.

The church, on which building work commenced in 1720, was designed by Isaac Wills. Little is known about him and it has been suggested that others may have also been involved in the design. While the planned, but not executed, elaborate and ornate west facade is credited to him, it was copied from two churches in Rome, from San Giacomo degli Incurabili for the west front and San Agnese in the Piazza Navona for the tower which was to surmount the front. Financial difficulties resulted in the completion of only a simplified version of the lower part while the upper part was left as a bare gable for nearly 150 years.

The remainder of the church was basilican in plan, with a rectangular hall and galleries on three sides, centre and side aisles and a curved apse with a shallow sanctuary at the east end, typical of Protestant churches of that period. The galleries are supported on unfluted Ionic columns. Other notable features are the single vault roof without the supports found in other similar churches, the rich deep plaster cornice [perhaps a later addition] and the six twelve feet long plaster drops [two of which may be later additions] flanking the windows in the apse.

With clear glass in the original classical nave windows, the interior of the church was bright. The beautiful organ case installed in the west gallery in 1742 still remains although a new organ replaced the original instrument almost a century later. The curved shelves in the apse on which bread was placed for the poor are a reminder that the eighteenth century church was surrounded by very poor housing. It was not always the fashionable church it was to become in the following century and for a period of time it was called 'dirty St. Ann's'.

A plan by Murray for the completion of the west front with a tower and spire was exhibited at the Royal Hibernian Academy in 1828 but not implemented. Some repairs were carried out in 1835 and a bell made by Hodges, Sackville St., Dublin, was installed in 1842, but there was little change until the long incumbency of Hercules Dickinson [1855-1902]. The ground floor plan of the church, drawn in 1859 by Joseph Welland as a prelude to reordering of the interior fittings, records the traditional pattern of classical churches. The altar was placed against the wall in the apse with a combined three-decker pulpit, reading and parish clerk's desks situated in the central aisle at the east end of the nave in which there were box pews.

During the re-ordering in 1859-1860, the box pews, the canopied pews of the Archbishop of Dublin and the Duke of Leinster in the galleries and the three-decker were removed, a new pulpit, of Caen stone, and reading desk were installed in changed positions, the choir was moved from the west gallery to the chancel and four segmental-headed window openings were made under the galleries on both north and south walls. The original reredos, a pedimented aedicule, flanked by two panelled bays between Corinthian pilasters, was altered to fit a slight alteration to the apse. Two stained glass windows of dark Victorian glass installed at that time were followed by seven more over a period of five years.

These interior changes were followed in 1868 by plans for the construction of a new west front to be set forward from the original façade. In the plans the bare upper gable and the simplified Italianate lower front were hidden by a new 'polychrome and subtly asymmetrical Lombardo Romanesque façade' [Williams] designed by Deane and Woodward. The tall central gable wall, on which a gabled portal was surmounted by a miniature arcade and a wheel window, was flanked by two towers of differing heights, one of which was to be a campanile with bells. For a second time a western façade planned for the church was not completed fully as the construction of the higher northern tower did not reach the belfry stage and was covered with a simple conical cap.

The installation of stained glass windows of sombre colours, the preferred choice of the Victorians, made the interior dark. The stained glass, perhaps the penalty of being a rich and fashionable church, has been described as 'very ugly' and 'nearly all of it execrable' [Craig] yet he considered St. Ann's remained one of the noblest churches in Dublin. The increasing height and close proximity of buildings around the church in the twentieth century darkened the interior further yet it has been argued that the loss of light has been compensated for to some extent by the resulting peaceful and reflective atmosphere.

It has also been said that some of the Victorian windows are more notable for whom they commemorate than for their quality yet the five early windows by O'Connor have been described as a remarkable achievement [Williams]. The early twentieth century windows in the south aisle by Wilhemina Geddes, of the internationally renowned An Tur Gloine co-operative, are held to be of particular note. The patron saint of the church is depicted, together with St. Mark, in the most recent window [1979] in the upper north wall. In the vestry there is a cartoon, by Evie Hone, for a proposed window depicting St. Ann which was not commissioned.

The church is also noteworthy for the large number of memorial tablets which, it has been said, add nothing to its beauty and perhaps even disfigure the church to some extent especially those with extravagant and eulogistic inscriptions. Among those remembered are Sir Hugh Lane, the famous art collector, Archbishop Whateley of Dublin and Alexander Knox, 'a major but unrecognised theologian'. One famous person not remembered in glass or stone is Thomas Barnardo, the philanthropist, who attended the parish Sunday School. Theobald Wolfe Tone, held to be the father of Irish Republicanism and co-founder of the United Irishmen, married Martha Witherington, a parishioner, in the church in 1785.

In 1902 the three central panels of the reredos were filled with Venetian mosaic as a memorial to Hercules Dickinson, Rector 1855-1902. Two further panels were added in 1920 as a memorial to parishioners who had died in World War I. The roof was replaced in 1911 and the cornice may have been added at that time. Some years later the Caen stone pulpit, installed in 1859, was replaced and the south aisle became a lady chapel. A major restoration was carried out in 1964 during which the cornice was highlighted, the plaster drops in the apse were redecorated with gold leaf and the eighteenth century organ case in the west gallery was decorated in striking white and gold colours. In 1973 the century old west façade was cleaned revealing the complementary colours of the old red sandstone, Portland stone, limestone and Wicklow granite used.

Throughout much of its life St. Ann's has been seen by parishioners as a fashionable church but it has also been an important incumbency in the Church of Ireland being a stepping stone for promotion of clergy. Seventeen of the twenty four incumbents prior to the present Rector became senior dignitaries of the church, nine to bishoprics, of whom one became an archbishop, and eight were appointed to important deaneries or archdeaconries.

Dublin, Dawson Street: St. Ann – 1868 plan

DUBLIN, ST. AUDOEN'S: ST. ANNE'S CHAPEL

St. Audoen's Church, Dublin, dedicated to St. Ouen, seventh century bishop of Rouen, was built between 1181 and 1212 during the episcopacy of John Comyn, the first Norman Archbishop of Dublin. Situated in the centre of mediaeval Dublin, the church gradually became an important part of the religious, civic and commercial life of the city. It is the only remaining mediaeval parish church in Dublin.

Dublin, St. Audoen: St.
Anne's Chapel
Fresco discovered 1887

During mediaeval times the desire of many in the Western Church to ensure the safe arrival of their soul in Heaven led to the establishment of chantries. Many were simple endowments providing money for a priest to say or chant masses for the souls of the deceased founder at any church but other endowments also provided for the foundation and maintenance of chantry chapels.

In 1430 Henry VI signed the royal warrant granting permission for the building at St. Audoen's of a chantry chapel, 'in praise of God and the Blessed Virgin Mary and in honour of St. Anne', for a lay organisation which was to be called 'The Guild and Fraternity of St. Anne'. The chapel, which most likely replaced an earlier and narrower aisle of the church, was built on the south side of the nave of St. Audoen's into which it opened through five arches. The chapel contained six altars, one being dedicated to St. Anne, at which priests said masses for the departed members of the Guild. Permission was granted to the Guild to acquire land to provide an income for maintaining the chantry. Over many years the Guild obtained possession of a large amount of property, mainly from bequests by deceased members, in the area around St. Audoen's.

Unlike the English chantries, those in the parish churches in Ireland were not included in the 1547 legislation and therefore the guild was not dissolved. St.Audoen's, together with St. Anne's Chapel, passed to the Church of Ireland at the Reformation but the Chapel continued to be used by the Guild whose members were recusants. Throughout the seventeenth century there were several unsuccessful attempts by leaders of church and state to curb the wealth and power of St. Anne's Guild.

Eventually in 1695 after a century of dispute mainly about the use of the Guild income, a bill was passed which dissolved the chantries in Ireland including that maintained by St. Anne's Guild. The chapel was then used as part of St. Audoen's Parish Church although it is likely that some alterations would have been made to the fittings to make it more appropriate for worship in the Church of Ireland tradition.

Due to a declining congregation the roof was removed, in the 1770s, from the part of the church located to the east of both St. Audoen's nave and St. Anne's Chapel. Further decline in congregation numbers led, in 1820-1821, to the removal of the roof of St. Anne's Chapel. The arches leading into the nave of the church were built up and the chapel was abandoned to the elements. Much later in the nineteenth century the distinguished architect Thomas Drew provided detailed plans of the church and made the first serious attempt to draw attention to its historical and architectural importance [Crawford].

The chapel was roofed again in 2002 by the Office of Public Works and it is now a visitor centre and exhibition space, with steel galleries against north and west walls, portraying the importance of St. Audoen's in the life of Medieval Dublin. The built up arcade on the north wall is partly exposed but the moulded pointed arches between the chapel and nave and the composite piers on which they rest are best seen from the parish church. Above the modern doorway in the south east corner, and best seen from the exterior, there is a large four light sandstone window which was built in the fifteenth century using materials from an earlier window, perhaps from the original narrower aisle. This window was reconstructed and placed in its original position by the Office of Public Works. The south wall, of uncoursed limestone, bears the evidence of much alteration during the long history of the chapel.

There are a number of architectural features which suggest how the chapel was used prior to the dissolution of the Irish chantries. On the south wall there are a few arched recesses, the largest of which contained an altar. A wall painting, possibly of St. Anne and the Holy Trinity or perhaps the Blessed Virgin Mary, was discovered in a recess during work on the chapel walls in 1887. It has been suggested that the painting, which may have been from as early as the thirteenth century, was painted to resemble a three-light window. According to some sources it was painted over soon after discovery but it may have simply deteriorated through exposure to the elements. There is a small pointed arched doorway framed in dressed sandstone which opened to a narrow cobbled lane leading to a priest's house. Squint windows high on the south wall, through which an altar could be seen, suggest that the priest's house abutted the chapel at first floor level.

EASKEY: ST. ANNE

St. Anne's Parish Church, in the Diocese of Killala, is situated in the village of Easkey [Iascaigh – abounding in fish] on the remote West Sligo coastline. The small church, with an attractive tower and spire rising above the churchyard elms, overlooks the Easkey River as it enters the Atlantic Ocean.

The parish, then named Imelachisial, was first mentioned in records in 1307 and the first vicar in 1413. The mediaeval parish church, which passed to the Church of Ireland at the Reformation, stood in the village on a different but as yet unknown site from the later church. It was recorded, under the parish name Imlaghishell als Icskegh, as being in use at the 1615 Royal Visitation. Just over a century and a half later it was decided to replace that church. The Order in Council, dated 10 May 1768, stated that 'the ancient church of Easkey being thought improper to be rebuilt and a new church being proposed to be built in a more convenient place on part of ye glebe land ..... conveyed by Rev James Hutchinson, Vicar of the parish to the churchwardens for ever for building a new church thereon ..... to be the parish church of Easkey for ever'.

There is no extant written record of the dedication of either the mediaeval or c.1768 church in the parish or other apparent evidence of the mediaeval cult of St. Anne in the area but the ancient chalice, still in use, is engraved with the date 1753 and the dedication to 'St. Ann [sic]'. This might suggest that the dedication was passed on from the mediaeval church but it is also possible that, prior to that year, the church may have been given that name in memory of Queen Anne. Her remission of First Fruit funds from the Crown to the Church of Ireland helped to build several churches in the Province of Tuam in the eighteenth century, perhaps including Easkey.

Although there is no record of the actual date of building or description of the fabric of the new eighteenth century parish church, it was this building which was destroyed or damaged beyond repair during the 1798 Rebellion. This probably took place after General Humbert landed with French troops at Killala in August of that year and a Connacht Republic was briefly established. The vicar of Easkey, James Moore, is recorded as having lost property worth £375 in the rebellion.

The present church, dating from 1820 and erected on the foundations and incorporating the tower of the c. 1768 building, is not liturgically orientated with the east end facing south. It has most of the architectural features of a typical early nineteenth century Board of First Fruits design but with the addition of shallow transepts which make it cruciform in shape. A vestry was added at a later date on the [liturgical] south east corner. The windows, with the exception of the large stained glass east window, are pointed with Y-tracery and square panes of clear glass in wooden frames. The two stage tower has a string-course and hood mouldings on the louvred openings. It is surmounted by a battlemented parapet with pinnacles at the corners and a slender octagonal spire. All openings on the building have dressed stone surrounds and the walls are harled in pebbledash.

The building was financed by a loan of £1342 [Lewis] or £1238 [Parliamentary Gazetteer] from the Board of First Fruits and annual repayments required by this large amount together with the interest was to impose a heavy burden on the funds of the parish for many years. The minutes of the Vestry throughout the nineteenth century record the constant battle to repair the church from the effects of high rainfall, damp conditions and its constant exposure to frequent storms blowing in from the ocean. The bills for repairs increased towards the end of the century as the fabric deteriorated.

In 1878 the church was closed and the courthouse in the village used for services as repairs were made to the roof, stonework, floors and pews. Another major repair to the roof was necessary in 1886. It became evident after two violent storms in the early twentieth century that a major restoration of the entire building was urgently needed. After a lengthy period of closure, the church was re-opened for worship in the summer of 1912 but three years later a further major repair to the spire, the oldest part of the building, was necessary.

Over the years, in addition to the constant repairs, the church has been adorned. The old wooden pulpit and reading desk were replaced in the late nineteenth century by new fittings made of alabaster and marble of typical late Victorian design. In 1945, a beautiful stained glass east window, depicting Jesus Christ as the Light of the World, was commissioned from Kitty O'Brien of An Tur Gloine. Fourteen years later a new baptistery was consecrated.

Towards the end of the twentieth century it again became obvious that another very major restoration of the church was necessary. A savings fund, which had been opened in the 1980s, became a major restoration appeal for £90,000 in 1997. With generous support from the local community, throughout Ireland and overseas, the work commenced in 2002. The major exterior restoration consisted of extensive work on the roof, tower, walls and drainage from the building and around the church. The bell, which has no date or inscription, had fallen from its frame but was saved from major damage and falling to the ground floor of the tower by the accumulated rooks' nests underneath. It has been restored, rehung and now rings again for services.

Major interior restoration included replacement of the wooden floor, window frames and wainscoting and work on the walls, the east window and the vestry. At the west end a shallow gallery, which had been removed many years ago, was replaced. The new gallery, to which access is gained from a stone staircase rising from the porch, is supported on beams. The chancel stretches into the crossing from the east end where the raised sanctuary is enclosed by an elliptical communion rail. Overhead the new pine roof is supported by a structure which has both hammer beam and king post features.

The beautifully restored and decorated church was rededicated in November 2004 when the whole local community gathered for a celebration of the re-opening. It is inspiring to visit St. Anne's and see the restoration of a much cherished church by a small congregation with the generous support of their neighbours and others further afield.

Easkey: St. Anne

ENNISKILLEN: ST. ANNE *(until 1923)*

In 1611, during the Ulster Plantation, Captain William Cole was granted land on Enniskillen [Inis Ceithleann – Ceithleann's Island], an island on the River Erne, by King James. Cole was required by the conditions of the grant to build a town on the island and bring 20 British families to settle there and for whom he had to build a church. The dates of commencement and completion of the building are not known with certainty but erection may have started with the appointment of the first rector in 1622. It was built on the more western and higher of the two hills on the island.

Not much is known about this church and there is no extant contemporary illustration. It was described as being 20 feet long and roofed with shingles which were replaced by slates in 1735. It seems to have had a T-shape with a nave and integral chancel, a shallow transept on the north wall and, on the opposite south wall, the pulpit, reading desk, clerk's desk and font extending out to the central aisle. The church also had a western tower to which a low spire, pyramidal or hexagonal according to different sources, was added in 1721. The spire was increased in height at a later date but removed, because of instability, in 1832.

Changes were made to the interior of this church as the population of the parish increased. A number of separate galleries were built of which at least one was for private use and another to accommodate soldiers from the British Army Garrison. By 1801, when a further new gallery was built for soldiers, the galleries extended along three sides of the church. It does not seem to have been a satisfactory building as the Vestry Minutes record the need for continual maintenance and frequent repairs. In the *OS Memoirs* of the parish it is described as being building with no architectural beauty. The Vestry considered another extension in 1826 but with increasing population and the poor state of the building it became obvious that a complete rebuild was necessary.

The new building, consecrated on 7 June 1842, is in Perpendicular style introduced into Ireland in the early nineteenth century by the Pain brothers, Board of First Fruits architects. It is not certain who designed the church. Local sources suggest it was Thomas Elliott of Ballyconnell but architectural historians believe it was more likely to have been William Farrell, Ecclesiastical Commissioners Architect for the Province of Armagh with Elliott acting as contractor.

The only parts of the earlier church which, it is generally agreed, were incorporated in the new building were the tower, albeit remodelled, clad and raised in height, traces of a chamfered arch on its east wall, the eighteenth century main church door with a small three-light window above and a stone, with the date 1637 and a carving of the Paschal Lamb, set in the wall of the tower. There are, however, features on the west wall of the north aisle which suggest it may have been part of an eighteenth century north transept mentioned in some sources. The traces of an infilled round-headed opening above the door leading to the belfry, the separate hipped roof hidden by the parapet, the quoins and stone work and dressings are reminiscent of other eighteenth century churches in Fermanagh, such as Aghalurcher.

The much wider nave and side aisles of the new building are offset from the tower and as a result the entrance to the church is in the corner of the south aisle. The clerestoried nave and side aisles are of six bays with Y-tracery windows and, on the south side facing the main street of the town, shallow buttresses which are surmounted by finials matching those on the tower. The tower was lowered by several feet to remove unstable parts and was then increased in height commencing at the level of the label stops on the belfry windows. It was then encased in shallow Perpendicular features, topped with quatrefoil banding and surmounted by a thin octagonal spire.

The interior of the building is described as being light and delicate and characteristically Late Georgian rather than Early Victorian [Rowan]. The side aisles, each with their own pitched roof and shallow vaulting, are divided from the nave by arcades of low perpendicular arches supported on quatrefoil columns. The galleries, which run along three walls of the nave, are also supported on the columns. Above the arches the windows in the clerestory pierce the ribbed vaulting of the ceiling.

In 1889 the initial shallow chancel was extended, in keeping with dimensions of the 1842 building, to accommodate stalls for a diocesan chapter thus providing an early indication of the desire for cathedral status. The 1856 stained glass east window, depicting four Resurrection subjects, was relocated to the new east window position. The wooden front panels on the galleries were cut to form balustrades and painted white to lighten the interior of the church. The double-decker pulpit, which may have come from the old church, was replaced. It had stood in the centre of the church at the east end but the new pulpit was located on the north side.

The chancel was refitted and the east end reordered in 1923, when the church was raised to cathedral status. The architect was Richard Caulfeild Orpen, one of two architects who had designed St. Anne's, Rahan. The organ, which had been in the west gallery, was replaced by a new instrument located in the north-east corner and a new vestry was added on the south-east corner. The area between the organ and new vestry was raised and formed into a choir also with chapter stalls and the sanctuary was panelled with coloured marble.

The cathedral contains the colours and memorials of the two famous regiments, the Royal Inniskilling Fusiliers and the Royal Inniskilling Dragoons, connected with the town. When they ceased to exist in 1968, the Regimental Association requested that a Chapel should be made for them in the Cathedral. The chapel, dedicated a few years later, was created by removing one bay of the north gallery, roofing two bays of the aisle with a suspended ceiling of cedar and separating it from the nave by a wrought iron screen. Those changes have been described as 'unhappy' [Williams], 'difficult to look at with approval' [Brett] and containing 'an ill-proportioned and impractical altar' [Galloway].

There are other interesting memorials in the cathedral. Among those are a 1628 gravestone tablet, which is now set in the west wall of the nave, the classical octagonal shaped font presented by a rector in 1666 and life size monuments of two early nineteenth century members of the Enniskillen family of Florencecourt. The attractive Gothic Revival case of the early nineteenth century organ, which was removed in 1923, still stands in the west gallery.

The original bell, first mentioned in a 1677 record, was replaced in 1716 by two bells, named William and Mary, which are said to have been made from Irish cannon taken by King William's Army at the Battle of the Boyne. These bells were recast, in 1828, into one bell which later became the sixth of a chime of eight bells installed in the new church in 1842. In 1935 these eight bells were removed and with the addition of two treble bells were hung for full-circle ringing and striking the quarters and hours.

Galloway states that the early seventeenth century church was dedicated to St. Anne at its completion in 1637 but does not provide the source. There is no extant evidence in early records or on inscriptions on early church plate to support the 1637 date. Duke states that the dedication to St. Anne was first given to the new church in 1842 but again no source is stated. If 1842 is the correct date then it is possible that it was named in memory of Anne Isabella, Viscountess Hawarden, the mother of the Revd. and Honourable John Maude, Rector [1824 –1860] at the building of the church.

The dedication to St. Anne was first listed in the Irish Church Directory in 1917. Four years later a bill to create a second cathedral for the diocese at Enniskillen was introduced and passed in the General Synod, despite the existence of the ancient site and diocesan cathedral at Clogher. This resulted in 'an abrupt, confusing and unnecessary change of dedication' to St. Macartin [Galloway], with no known reason for the slightly different spelling. Further confusion was caused at the General Synod in 1923 with an unsuccessful attempt by Lord Belmore to change the name to St. Fergus, the dedication of the first post-Reformation parish church which was situated on Iniskeen Island. Curiously, but unsurprisingly given the poor record keeping of the Church of Ireland, the dedication of the church/cathedral to St. Anne remained in the Irish Church Directory until 1924.

Enniskillen: St. Anne (now St. Macartin)

KILBARRON: ST. ANNE

St. Anne's, Kilbarron [Cill Barrain – the church of St. Barrain], in the Diocese of Raphoe, is situated above the town of Ballyshannon, Co. Donegal, on the historic hill of Mullaghnashee, with majestic views across the Lower Erne Valley to the mountains in Leitrim and North Sligo.

There is a tradition that the mediaeval parish church at Creeny was established by St. Columba with his cousin, St. Barrain, as bishop. This ancient church may have been used by British settlers in the early seventeenth century but a new church, situated more conveniently for parishioners living in the small town, was built on Mullaghnashee by 1622 at the latest. A baptismal font, octagonal in shape with a square shaft, which was installed in that church in 1700 was found in a house in the town in the late nineteenth century. Perhaps it had been removed when that church was demolished in 1735. It was being used for feeding ducks when it was discovered by the rector who restored it to the parish church.

By the 1730s the shingle-roofed building had become very dilapidated and a new church was built in 1735 on a site to the west of the old building. The church was cruciform in shape and dedicated to St. Anne although no record of the date of the naming survives. It may have been the dedication of the mediaeval or the 1622 church but there is no documentary evidence of that. Alternatively, it is possible that it was named in memory of Queen Anne who had shown interest in the state of the established church in Ireland by remitting First Fruits and supporting legislation which made building of new churches much easier.

The prevailing damp conditions of the area and its exposure to strong winds blowing in from the Atlantic Ocean led yet again to the gradual deterioration of the fabric of the 1735 building. In the year of its centenary the Rural Dean's report recorded that the church and especially the roof and ceiling were in very bad repair. Part of the ceiling had collapsed during a service injuring some members of the congregation. The church was extensively damaged in the Great Wind of January, 1839 and a decision was taken to build a new church. Services had to be held elsewhere until the new church opened in 1841.

It was built on the same site by the Rector, Revd. G. N. Tredennick, to the design of William Farrell, the Ecclesiastical Commissioners' architect, in what has been described as the Saxon Style of architecture [Rowan]. With its situation on the hill above the town and the harled walls painted white it is a very distinctive landmark in the area. It is a large five-bay, two storey hall with a high roof which to some extent reduces the impact of the high four-stage west tower. A tall chancel extends eastwards from the hall and there is a low single storey vestibule with battlemented parapet on the south-east corner.

Apart from the four-stage tower, which may be a remnant of the 1735 church, it is built of ashlar sandstone with wide strips of dressed stone masonry beneath the eaves, between bays and at corners. The windows, round-headed in the upper storey and segmental-headed below the galleries, have two lights, stone mullions and dressed stone surrounds and are recessed on the areas of wall between the vertical masonry strips.

The round-headed door with arches of dressed stone on the south facing tower wall is dwarfed by the height of the rather plain tower on which the final two stages are slightly stepped. There is a clock face and double round-headed louvred openings on each of the four faces of the third and fourth stages, respectively. Above the final belfry stage the tower is topped with battlements in Irish style. The belfry contains a carillon of eight bells installed in 1903 to replace an earlier ring from 1884.

Inside, the church is high and spacious and beautifully decorated and maintained. There are original box pews on either side of the central aisle in the nave. The galleries, which run along three sides, have pierced wooden panelled fronts and are supported on cast iron columns with decorated capitals. They were installed in 1891 to accommodate soldiers from the British Army Garrison at nearby Finner Camp. The walls are plastered and above there is a ceiling of wooden panelling with a cornice-like decorative surround.

Alterations were made to the interior of the church in 1900. The chancel, which is raised on three steps, was remodelled and tiled. Beautiful stained glass windows, depicting the Resurrection, the Sermon on the Mount and the Ascension, by Percy Bacon of London, were installed in the large three-light east window. The choir stalls were moved out beyond the chancel arch to the east end of the nave and the 1860 organ was enlarged and moved from the west gallery to the north-east corner of the nave. A new pulpit, in memory of the long serving rector who had recovered the ancient font, and matching reading desk of Caen Stone, alabaster and marble, in typical late Victorian style, were dedicated. It is probable that the box pews in the side aisles may have been replaced at that time. Ten years later in 1910, the chancel was further adorned when a carved oak reredos and oak panelling were installed.

The exposed position of the church on a hill was highlighted again in September 1961 when Hurricane Debbie blew in from the ocean causing much damage to the church and tower and requiring extensive repairs over a period of time. A further major restoration was carried out in 1994 after which the church was rehallowed.

There is a fine, interesting and varied collection of memorials on the interior walls including one to a Napoleonic War veteran with a draped urn sitting above the instruments of the battlefield. There is also a cluster of six tablets in memory of members of the Stubbs family, who, over many years, were most generous benefactors in their frequent gifts to adorn the church, including both sets of bells and the stained glass in the east window. Outside in the churchyard there is a simple memorial to William Allingham, the poet, who wrote the ballad, 'The Winding Banks of Erne'. He was baptised at St. Anne's in 1824 but left Ballyshannon in 1846 to return only once, on the occasion of the funeral of his father. The urn containing the poet's ashes is buried in the churchyard.

Kilbarron: St. Anne

KILGLASS: ST. ANNE

The roofless and rapidly decaying Kilglass Parish Church is situated in the Diocese of Ardagh on a narrow country road five miles south of Edgeworthstown, Co. Longford. The earliest extant record of the parish is dated 1396 but there is no evidence of the existence of a mediaeval parish church. The adjoining parishes of Rathreagh and Ahara were united with Kilglass [Cille Glais – the grey church] to form the Kilglass Union in 1737. There is no record of a post-Reformation parish church in any of the three parishes of the union prior to the construction of St. Anne's, Kilglass.

Work on the construction of the small parish church, which may occupy the site of an ancient nunnery, began a few years before the formation of a Parish Vestry in 1813. Progress in building appears to have been slow owing to the financial difficulties of the three parishes which were thinly populated by members of the Church of Ireland. The total cost of the proposed building was £989 of which £339 was to be funded by a surprisingly small loan from the Board of First Fruits with the remaining £659 to be funded by parochial assessment. The minutes of the first ten years of the Annual Vestry Meetings record financial problems which were to remain continuously throughout the life of the church. In 1813 parishioners were required to provide their own pews and in the following two years there were difficulties in getting the church finished by the contractor.

It is most likely that building was completed in 1815 but there is no extant record of the consecration or dedication of the church. Progress continued to be slow and rough coating and whitewashing of the tower and remainder of the church was not completed until 1822 and 1823 respectively. The first renovation of the church took place over several years in the 1860s during which the parishioners provided a stationary font for the first time and the box pews were replaced with thirteen bench pews on either side of the centrally-placed aisle. The slow pace of the renovation resulted from the continuing financial problems. From 1876 the parish was never out of debt again and required continued financial assistance from diocesan and central church funds.

By the late 1880s there was growing concern among the parishioners about the future of the church. The financial concern was exacerbated by emigration of parishioners. In 1890 the Vestry decided not to build the proposed chancel but to concentrate on a thorough repair of the roof, church and windows. It was also decided to open three windows on the north wall of the nave. The work, which included the replacement of the roof, was not completed until 1912 but the decision to open three windows on the north wall was never implemented, presumably for financial reasons.

Further major renovation, including the tiling of the floors, took place in 1928 and electricity was installed in 1956 soon after becoming available in rural areas.

The final listing of the church in the Church of Ireland Directory was in 1996. Sadly, apart from the early Vestry Minutes, there are very few records of the church throughout its life. It would appear, from an unsuccessful search, that no photographic or written records of the exterior and interior of the church, when still in use for worship, were made at parish, diocesan or central church levels and no records of the final services exist.

The considerable growth of ivy since its closure makes it difficult to see clearly all features of the building. It is composed of a simple small rectangular hall with a centrally-placed western tower flanked at the ground stage by side vestibules. The tower contained a small bell on which there was no date or inscription. Although one source states there was an apsidal chancel there is no evidence of this on the ruin. The walls, where exposed underneath the rendering and ivy, are of random rubble with rough quoins on some corners. Typical of the period of building, there are no windows on the north wall.

The walls of the vestibules and lower stage of the tower are similar to the nave walls but the upper or belfry stage is of squared rubble. There are pointed windows, originally filled with timber Y-tracery but now with breeze blocks, on the western walls of the vestibules. The pointed entrance doorway, with finely worked dressed stone surround and hood moulding on which there are uncarved label stops, is now similarly infilled. The upper stage of the tower, which was not rendered, is the only slightly decorated part of an otherwise very simple building with broad string courses of dressed stone above and below the recessed louvred openings. The tower is topped with battlements and coping stones with slightly chamfered pyramidal pinnacles on the corners.

It could not be claimed that St. Anne's Kilglass was anything other than a rather plain Board of First Fruits church of the early nineteenth century with a few simple adornments on the west façade and tower. It is surely wrong, however, that it has been allowed by parochial, diocesan and central church authorities to descend into barely recorded oblivion.

Kilglass: St. Anne

KILLANE: ST. ANNE

St. Anne's, Killanne, in the Diocese of Ferns, is situated on the edge of the village of Killanne [Cill Aine – Anne's Church] in beautiful wooded countryside near the foot of the Blackstairs Mountain, Co. Wexford. The present church, consecrated in 1833, was built on a new site on the other side of the narrow country road from the mediaeval church.

There are no definite early records of the mediaeval building because of the difficulty in differentiating records of Killanne and Killegney Parishes. The Royal Visitation Report of 1615 recorded that Killane Church was being used for worship and the chancel was being repaired. This church was rebuilt in 1755/6, given a new roof in 1807 and further repaired in 1811. An application was made to the Board of First Fruits in 1825 for a loan of £600 to improve and enlarge the church but shortly afterwards the vestry resolved to build a new church and an application was made for a new loan of £1200.

Some of the materials of the old church, which was finally demolished in 1835, were used in construction of the new building. The Vestry Minutes state it was designed, in what contemporaries termed 'Early English Style', by Mr Rath. No further information has been found about the architect or other buildings designed by him. Although conforming broadly to the style of church building of the period with a three-bay rectangular hall and western tower, it differed from most Board of First Fruits designs for small rural churches of that period by having a small shallow structural chancel, north wall windows and more decorative external features.

Improvements were made periodically throughout the nineteenth century, a bell, made by Hodges, Sackville St., Dublin, was installed in 1841, a font in 1842, a stained glass window in the nave in 1868, a new reredos in 1878 and a new organ in 1894. The plaster ceiling was opened and roof timbers replaced, in 1886, with wooden panelling supported by composite roof trusses. A major restoration, financed by the Blacker and Beresford families, was carried out in 1901. The work included the building of a chancel arch of dressed stone, the lining of the limestone walls with plaster and the installation of gifts of a new oak pulpit, reading desk and reredos, stained glass for two of the three narrow lancets on the east wall and a tiled sanctuary floor.

Inside the church, the baptistery and organ are situated at the west end on either side of the carpeted centrally-placed aisle. At the other end of the nave the pulpit and reading desk are located to the west of the chancel arch outside the shallow sanctuary area. The windows on the north wall and one on the south wall of the nave have original metal frames and are glazed with diamond panes of clear glass. Two on the south wall have stained glass, one of which dates from 1914 and was made by Powell and Sons, the famous London firm. The stained glass in the third lancet in the sanctuary, depicting the 'The Good Shepherd', was designed and made, in 1938, by Catherine O'Brien of An Tur Gloine.

The exterior of the church is constructed of roughly dressed limestone in broadly horizontal courses with four buttresses on both nave walls. There is a wide low buttress below the triple lancets, the central of which is taller, on the gable wall of the chancel, which has a lower roof and is narrower than the nave. All openings on the building are pointed and those on the north and south walls are recessed. Those on the two stage stepped tower are deeply recessed with gently inward-sloping reveals and hood mouldings. There is a surprisingly narrow louvred lancet on each of the four faces on the belfry stage of the tower. Above this the tower is surmounted by pinnacles at each corner and small gabled parapets each decorated with an incised cross, all topped with matching finials.

The site of the former church and the adjoining old parish graveyard are situated on the other side of the road. Until 1866 this graveyard was the common burial ground for the parish and many of those from Killane who died during the 1798 rebellion were buried in a separate plot. One of the leaders of the rebellion commemorated there is John Kelly, whose name and deeds have been made famous by the song, 'Kelly the Boy from Killanne', but he was not buried in the graveyard. Having been seriously injured at the Battle of Ross in early June, he was executed at Wexford. His head was then cut off and spiked and his body was thrown into the river.

Little more is known about John Kelly but there is evidence to support the belief that he and his family were parishioners of St. Anne's, Killanne. His father, also John Kelly, is recorded in the Vestry Minute Books as a churchwarden for a number of years between 1777 and 1796 and by the record, in the parish burial register, of his death on 20 September 1797. The Vestry Minute Books also record that his son John Kelly attended a meeting of the Vestry on 17 April 1798 and handed a sum of money to the parish in memory of his father. Both father and son would have known the Reverend Pentland, the curate of the parish, who, aged twenty two, was piked and killed by rebels at the Battle of Vinegar Hill despite the efforts of a Roman Catholic rebel from the parish to save him.

There is no record of the dedication of the church to St. Anne but there can be little doubt that it took place in mediaeval times when the cult of St. Anne spread to Ireland. The name of the townland is an indication of the antiquity of the dedication. Further proof is afforded by St. Anne's Holy Well which is located at the far end of the field adjoining the old graveyard. The well was the focus of the annual pattern, patronal feast day, on 26th July but this was abolished by the Roman Catholic Church in 1824 because of the behaviour of many pilgrims. It is still a place of pilgrimage and prayer to St. Anne as can be seen by the modern votive offerings on the surrounding bushes.

Killane: St. Anne

KILLOUGH: ST. ANNE

St. Anne's Killough, Co. Down, originally in the parish of Rathmullan, Diocese of Down, is a small plain church surrounded by trees and a low sea wall beside a sheltered and shallow bay on the Irish Sea coastline. It is situated at the end of a tree-lined avenue leading from the formally arranged Palatine Square in the village. Although the Lecale Peninsula was the core of the Norman settlement in Ulster there is no record of an early church or settlement at Killough. There was a church on the site in 1713, according to the map by John Sloane, and probably for many years before that. Records indicate that there was a small settlement at Killough from the early seventeenth century but no church was recorded there in the 1657 Inquisition of the Dioceses of Down, Connor and Dromore.

Sir Robert Ward, who purchased the village and surrounding land from the Earl of Kildare in 1671, probably built the original church sometime in the late seventeenth century. It was replaced or rebuilt, circa 1716, as a chapel of ease to the parish church situated more than four miles distant. Nothing is known of this building except that it was described, in 1744, as being a 'decent church'. By the 1790s it was in very poor repair and the Revd. John Hamilton, Rector of Rathmullan, who died in 1797, bequeathed £200 for the purpose of rebuilding it.

The new chapel of ease built in 1802 is substantially the basis of the present church with some modifications and additions. The architect is unknown but it was built to a Board of First Fruits design, with a four-bay rectangular hall and west tower with flanking vestibules, typical of the early nineteenth century churches found in different dioceses throughout Ireland. Perhaps uniquely the octagonal spire was made of wood but having been seriously damaged in the Great Wind of 1839 it fell through the roof. Major repairs had to be carried out to the church and tower in addition to the replacement of the spire which took place around 1842. The inscription on the tower bell, made by Thomas Hodges, Abbey St., Dublin, is 'Bequest of the Revd. John Hamilton to Killough Church 1796: obtained by the incumbent 1858'.

Over thirty years later a further major restoration was needed. The church was reopened on 16 July 1876 after work which included the replacement of the old box pews with bench pews, the installation of a new pulpit, reading desk and communion rail and renewal of gallery woodwork. At an unrecorded date in the late nineteenth century, a chancel was added reflecting the increasing emphasis on the sacraments in worship. Further changes were the remodelling of the chancel and sanctuary in 1915 and the addition of a vestry on the north east corner in 1932.

It is a simple church with few decorative features on the exterior fabric. The rubble walls have been rendered and there are quoins on the tower and west gable wall. In keeping with most churches of the early nineteenth century there are no windows on the north wall. Those on the south wall have Y-tracery with stone mullions, diamond shaped panes of opaque glass and dressed stone surrounds which have been painted.

The three-stage tower has yellow brickwork in the upper courses which was probably added at the repair after the damage sustained in 1839. The stages are marked by string-courses, the upper one of which incorporates a hood moulding for the louvred openings on the belfry. The tower, which is topped with a pierced parapet and pinnacles on the corners, is surmounted by the replacement octagonal granite spire. At ground stage, the flanking vestibules have narrow lancets and the west door surround is of granite now painted.

Inside, the hall contains the nave and a small western gallery supported on two slim quatrefoil columns on either side of the centrally-placed aisle. The chancel is divided from the nave by an arch of dressed stone supported on single columns. The sanctuary is lit by a three-light window with stone mullions, intersecting tracery and a little stained glass with an Alpha and Omega design. There is also a narrow lancet on the south wall. Above the plastered walls, the wooden panelled roof of the nave is supported on king post trusses.

Outside in the churchyard, close to the gate, is the grave of Charles Sheil, a native of Killough, who made a large fortune in his shipping and trade businesses in Liverpool. Throughout his life he had a warm sympathy for the poor and on his death in 1861 he bequeathed £120,000 for the erection of almshouses, or Sheils Institutes as they were called, in Killough and four other towns, including one close to St. Anne's, Dungannon. The attractive almshouses in Killough were erected in 1868 on the edge of the village.

There is no extant record of the dedication of any of the three churches on the site. It is possible that the Ward family may have wanted the 1716 chapel of ease to be dedicated in memory of Queen Anne who died in 1714. It is much more likely, however, that Michael Ward, who created the village and port at Killough and gave it the name 'Port St. Anne', in the early eighteenth century in honour of his wife, Anne Hamilton, whom he married in 1709, also gave the same name to the church.

Killough: St. Anne

KILLULT: ST. ANN

Tullaghobegley [Tulacha Bheighile – Begley's little hill] is a very extensive parish situated in North West Donegal, in the Diocese of Raphoe. A substantial proportion of the parish is composed of mountain and bogland and it also includes Tory and some other islands off the coast. The mediaeval parish church, situated in Ballintemple townland [O'Ceallaigh], was in use in 1609 but in ruins at the Royal Visitation, 1622 [OS Memoirs], and at the Civil Survey, 1654. Eighty years later there was still no church in the parish at the c.1733 Visitation. No record survives of the dedication of the mediaeval parish church. Another source [Leslie] states there were five ancient churches in the parish.

A church was built for the parish in 1792 by the Board of First Fruits at a cost of over £369 but the location of the building is not named in any of the sources. Information in those sources is somewhat confusing and conflicting, but the 1792 church appears to have been replaced in 1820 by another church at Killult townland, which adjoins Ballintemple. It is also possible this may have been a total rebuild of the 1792 church. The new church was consecrated in June 1820 but there is no extant record of the dedication which in later records is named variably as both St. Ann and St. Anne.

In 1824 the rector, Evan Jenkins, stated that the church was in bad repair which suggests it may have been a rebuild of the 1792 building. Ten years later in 1834, 'the roof fell in' after which services were held for a time at the home of the rector which was a thatched cottage on glebe land below the church. The church was rebuilt in 1840 at a cost of £620 [Leslie] but the Parliamentary Gazetteer of 1844 stated it still had no roof although it would seem very likely this was a mistaken reference to another church building.

There is no record of the roof collapse or the subsequent restoration in the Vestry Minutes of 1834 or following years. There are regular references, however, to repairs especially to the roof, commencing in 1821, resulting from the effects of the high rainfall in the area and exposure to frequent storms. The minutes also record that the church initially had a spire, not mentioned in other sources, which was removed in 1824. The walls of the tower and church were harled and whitewashed in 1830 in an attempt to protect the fabric. The never ending repairs consumed a major proportion of the income of this small poor parish with a declining membership [54 on register in 1860] and concern was expressed regularly about its financial difficulties. The 1876 minutes gratefully recorded a generous donation from Christ Church, Leeson Park, Dublin.

By 1883 the church, although still used for worship, was in a very dilapidated state as a result of the cumulative effect of major 'mountain storms' and the inability of the 'poorest parish in the North of Ireland' to carry out necessary repairs. Rather surprisingly therefore, a vestry, of uncoursed rubble, was added on the north wall in 1886 and major repairs and improvements, including tiling of the chancel and aisle, were carried out at a combined cost of £560. There is no record of how this work was funded.

The church at Killult [Cill Ulta – the church of Ultan] is situated on a low hill, about one mile west of Falcarragh, overlooking Tory Sound. It is of typical early Board of First Fruits design in very simple Gothic Renewal style with a three-bay rectangular hall and integrated west tower, harled exterior and pointed openings. On both north and south walls of the nave there are tall narrow lancets with wide dressed stone surrounds and glazed with square panes of clear glass. The south wall windows have the original iron frames but those on the more exposed north wall are modern replacements. The tall three light east window, glazed in the same way, has double-Y-tracery. An octagonal finial surmounts the east gable wall.

The rather large stumpy tower is of two stages marked by string-courses of dressed stone. The openings on the ground stage, doors on north and south walls and a small window on the west, are surrounded by wide pointed recesses. There is a small blind recess above the door on the south wall. On the belfry stage there are louvred openings on three walls. The tower is topped with dressed coping stones and low pyramidal pinnacles at the corners. Perhaps the spire, which was demolished in 1824, would have made the tower more balanced in proportion to the remainder of the building.

The *Armagh Guardian* of 25 March 1845 reported that Queen Adelaide, the Queen Dowager, widow of King William IV, had 'been pleased to give £20 to assist in purchasing a bell for the parish church of Killult ...... on the memorial of Revd. David Irvine, Rector thereof, and the Revd. Mr. Norman, curate'. The Queen, after whom the Adelaide Hospital, Dublin, was named, was noted for the large proportion of her income which she gave to charitable causes. It would seem that the rector and curate, knowing of her generosity, petitioned her asking for help. There is no record of the petition, purchase or installation of the bell in the Vestry Minutes of that period.

The interior, which is small with seating for around 100, has an integral chancel, raised on one step, occupying one bay at the east end. The font is located in the aisle near the west door and there is a large stove for heating, with a chimney leading up to the roof, in the middle of the church. Four large candelabra are suspended from the king post roof trusses. The walls and the ceiling, between the rafters, are of plaster.

There is only one wall memorial in the church but some items of furniture and the Tau Cross, based on the Tory Island Cross, and candlesticks are also memorials. In the churchyard, there is a cluster of several interesting gravestone inscriptions to sailors whose bodies were washed ashore after perishing in the waters of Tory Sound and the Atlantic Ocean. They were from HMS Wasp, which struck rocks on Tory during a gale in 1884, and HMS Dunvegan, an armed merchant convoy escort, which was torpedoed 200 miles west of Donegal in August 1940. The memorials to three Dutch sailors, whose cargo ship, the Stolwijk, was torpedoed in December 1940, still stand but their remains were exhumed and returned to the Netherlands in 2000. James Simmons, the Ulster poet, is a more recent burial in the churchyard.

Killult: St. Ann

KNOCKNAREA: ST. ANNE

St. Anne's Knocknarea, in the Diocese of Elphin, is a beautiful small church located in the ancient small parish of Killaspugbrone, over five miles west of Sligo on the road to Strandhill. It is situated close to the shoreline in a most scenic area below Knocknarea, on the top of which, according to legend, is the burial place of Maeve, Queen of Connacht.

In the 1830s, Divine Services for members of the Church of Ireland living in the two small parishes in the area were held in private houses or in a small school somewhere close to the site of the present church. The proposal to build a church in the parish was made initially in 1835 and six years later fund-raising commenced. The appeal in 1841 was made to 'Protestants of the Empire' to build a church at the foot of Knocknarea [Cnoc na Riadh – variously translated as 'the hill of execution, of the moon and of the kings and the smooth hill'].

The main reasons given for building a new church were that it would provide a place of worship for Church of Ireland families in the Strandhill area who lived at a considerable walking distance from the nearest parish churches at Sligo and Ballysodare and who were also reluctant to attend either church because of the contrast of 'their rustic garb with that of the better clad citizens' of those towns.

By 1843 the required endowment of £1250 had been raised, almost all of which came from the local gentry who eventually were made trustees of the church. With further fund-raising by trustees and a grant from the Ecclesiastical Commissioners, work on the building commenced and the foundation stone of the building was laid on 29 September 1843. Almost two years later it was consecrated and dedicated to St. Anne, as shown on the inscription above the porch door, IN HONOREM B. ANNE DEO O.M. DEDICATA ERE PRIVATORUM COLLATO EDIFICATA A.D. MDCCCXLIII.

There is no extant record explaining the choice of dedication although as the wives and mothers of two of the most generous benefactors were both named Anne this may have been influential. The church was designed by John Benson, architect and engineer, of Sligo, who was later awarded a knighthood for his design of the buildings for the Irish Industrial Exhibition, Dublin, 1852.

The original small church was built in Gothic Revival style, with a three-bay nave, a lower and narrower structural chancel east of a chancel arch, a south facing porch and pointed openings. The nave was extended westwards by one bay in the mid 1860s with the architects, Welland and Gillespie, adhering to the design of the original building. The walls, apart from the north face, are of limestone ashlar which most likely came from quarries near Ballysodare. On the north face there are no windows, as in many other churches of that period, and the wall is rendered. The south, east and west walls which were visible from the old road have attractive features, with buttresses, hood mouldings on openings and tracery, stone mullions and dressed stone surrounds on the windows. The gable of the attractive porch on the south wall is pierced by a trefoil shaped decoration.

A stepped bell gable, containing a small bell with the inscription 'Sheridan, Dublin, 1843', surmounts the roof at the east end of the nave and there are small decorative features on the gable tops. The ridge tiles have a decorative motif and the roof has bands of patterned slates. Unfortunately the very attractive south face of the building is not seen as the improved road now runs to the north of the church exposing the rendered wall and a recently-built kitchen extension to passing traffic.

Inside, the church is simple and mainly glazed with diamond panes of clear glass but it contains several most attractive fittings and features. There is stained glass in the three-light east window [1873] depicting Biblical scenes, the lancet on the south wall of the sanctuary and the twin windows on the west wall which contain the coat of arms and crest of one of founding families of the church. The altar, of 'Neo-Elizabethan' design [Williams], the marble and alabaster reredos, the ornately carved granite font, the carved oak pulpit, chairs and roof trusses, the wooden panelled ceiling, and the beautifully carved corbels with angels painted in blue and gold are, perhaps, the most decorative features. The pews bear names scratched by pupils of Primrose Grange School which was situated in and had strong links with the parish until it moved in 1906 to become Sligo Grammar School.

There are many memorials in the church most of which commemorate members of the families of three original trustees whose interest and constant generosity has done much to ensure the continuing redecoration and repair of the fabric, to adorn the building and, in the nineteenth century, to augment the stipend of the rector. None of the descendents of those families now live in the parish but one maintains links and contributed very generously to the restoration of the church in the 1960s and gave a new organ in 1985. Many other families have also contributed over the years to the adornment and repair of the church.

There was a most painful dispute in the early 1920s when the bishop and the rector were taken to a consistorial court by a parishioner from one of those beneficent families for refusing him permission to lay the swords of his two sons, who had been killed in World War I, on their memorials. Permission was not granted on the theological grounds that there should be no sword in the sanctuary of a church and on the practical grounds that, in the disturbed state of the country at that time, they could be stolen and misused.

From 1681 until the disestablishment of the Church of Ireland in 1870, Killaspugbrone and Kilmacowen, the two small ancient parishes on the Strandhill peninsula, were united to and were a perpetual curacy within Sligo Parish. That union of parishes was dissolved in 1871 and St. Anne's became the parish church for the area but only for just over fifty years until 1923, when the parishes were united once again. Possible closure of St. Anne's, threatened for a period of time due to lack of clergy during a lengthy interregnum in the early 1980s, was thankfully avoided mainly due to the efforts of a lay reader who faithfully conducted Morning Prayer each Sunday during that time.

Knocknarea: St. Anne

MALLOW: ST. ANNE

The parish of Mallow [Maigh Ealla – the plain of the River Allo, the name given in mediaeval times to a stretch of the Blackwater] is situated in the Blackwater Valley, North Cork, in the Diocese of Cloyne. The earliest record of the parish is found in the 1307 Papal Taxation. There is another record from the same century of a fight inside the church between two priests both of whom claimed to be the rightful rector.

Although there was an earlier presence of Anglo-Normans in the area, the town of Mallow did not develop until the Tudor-Stuart period. It grew around the castle which commanded the important river crossing at this point. The mediaeval parish church, said to have been founded in the late twelfth century and dedicated to St Anne at an unknown date in mediaeval times, passed to the Church of Ireland at the Reformation. There is no extant record of the reason for the dedication but there appears to be little doubt that it resulted from Anglo-Normans bringing the cult of St. Anne to Ireland. It may have been the earliest dedication of a church to the saint in Ireland.

The church was damaged, repaired, extended and perhaps rebuilt on a number of occasions over the six centuries of its use for worship. After the Reformation it was damaged during the Nine Years War, 1593-1604, and in the 1641 Rebellion when insurgents occupied the town. The walls of the church suffered major damage during fighting in the area associated with the Williamite War but, after repairs, it was being used again for worship in 1694.

By 1817, however, the condition of the mediaeval building had deteriorated to such an extent that it was considered to be beyond repair. As a result it was decided to build a new church on land adjoining the ancient church and churchyard. The new church was consecrated in 1824 and dedicated to St. James and St. Anne's was closed for worship, the roof was removed and the building abandoned. It might have suffered a similar fate twenty five years earlier if a plot, by disaffected soldiers from the local garrison, to blow up the church with their officers inside at worship, had succeeded. After the old church was abandoned the ancient twelfth century baptismal font was brought to the new church where it is still used.

The abandoned, roofless and ruinous building still stands in the old overgrown churchyard, close to the 1824 parish church. Extant sources state that the building was repaired after being seriously damaged in 1691 but examination of the ruin clearly suggests that it was substantially rebuilt rather than simply being repaired. There is no extant record of any further work on the building during the eighteenth century so presumably it was rebuilt during the early 1690s.

The north and south nave and west gable walls, one metre in thickness and built of random rubble limestone, of the rectangular mediaeval church remain but the ruin contains features found in classical churches built at that period. On the south wall there are five round-headed windows with roughly dressed arches and rough quoins on the corners but, reminiscent of later Board of First Fruits churches, there are no openings on the north wall, which forms the boundary wall with adjoining properties. Most of the original east gable wall was replaced by a shallow apse squared-off on the exterior. A concave cornice and plain band, both of dressed stone, were added to the exterior of the south wall and around the apse but not on the north wall, the side which is not easily seen. The dressed stone corners of the squared-off apse remain but the east window opening and arch and wall above and below it have not survived. A ledge and joist holes and a door lintel above an infilled rectangular area in the shape and size of a doorway at first floor level on the east facing wall of the tower indicate the existence of a western gallery.

Although there is no extant record, the pre-Reformation church, as at not too distant Toem, had a western tower of three or perhaps four stages although it may have been a later addition to the original building. The three lower stages of the tower are, like the nave walls, of random rubble but the fourth stage is markedly different being of coursed random rubble with much larger roughly dressed stonework. This suggests that the tower was damaged in 1691 and the fourth stage was either added to the original three or rebuilt after damage. There are other features on the tower which suggest further additions were made during rebuilding. The dressed stone used for the two string-courses, the surrounds of the small rectangular windows on each of the faces of the third stage and the coping stones on the slightly battlemented tower are of the same stone and cut in similar short lengths.

According to local tradition, the bell in the old tower, which is rung for services at its successor church, did not belong originally to St. Anne's. There was, in an early act of ecumenical co-operation unconfirmed by records, an exchange of bells between the Roman Catholic and Church of Ireland parishes in 1900. After the construction of a new campanile at St. Mary's Roman Catholic Church it was found that the existing bell was not suitable. The bell from St. Anne's was given to St. Mary's where it still rings for services and in return the former St. Mary's bell was hung in St. Anne's tower. Alas, this local tradition is unfounded as shown by the inscription on the bell in St. Anne's tower which reads 'Cast at Gloucester by C & I Ruddall for the parish church of Mallow: The Revd William King Rector 1785'.

Among a number of famous people associated with St. Anne's were Thomas Davis, ᵗ Irish Patriot and the founder of the 'Young Ireland Movement' in 18. 'ised in the church in 1814 and Sir Richard Quain, baptised 181ᵗ after a brilliant medical career, became physician to Queen Victoɾ.

The St. ʌ 'storical Society was formed in January 1998 with the aim of bringin̹ ne's Church alive again for the people of Mallow' and visitors. It ̪ ed to create a park within the graveyard, to stabilise the ruin and resᵗ provide a Visitors' and Exhibition Centre for Mallow and surroundiᵗ Funding problems mean that those plans are now in abeyance.

Mallow: St. Anne

ERRATUM KILLANE in the Table of Contents p.III and in the Title on p.53 should read KILLANNE

MEENGLASS: ST. ANNE

The Church of the Ascension, Meenglass [Muine Glas ... the green mountain pasture/meadow] is located a few miles south of Stranorlar, in East Donegal, in the Diocese of Raphoe. Hidden from the road by forest plantation, it is situated in the townland of Carrickmagrath in a small clearing on a hillside above the Finn Valley. It is not the first church on the site, having replaced, in 1962, an earlier church dedicated to St. Anne.

The original church, consecrated on 12 October 1858, was built at the expense of James Hewitt, 4th Viscount Lifford, who also donated the piece of land from his large estate on which it was erected. The deed of consecration, one of the very few of that period to survive, had been lost but was discovered by the Bishop of Meath in a book in his library in 1943. It is now in the Derry and Raphoe Diocesan Papers in the Public Record Office of Northern Ireland.

The deed states that the church, to be dedicated to St. Anne, would be a chapel of ease in Donaghmore Parish. The 1856 Faculty granted permission for erection of the chapel to provide a convenient place of worship for those parishioners in the Meenglass area, which was over eight miles distant from the parish church situated at Castlefinn. There is no indication in the deed or in any extant contemporary records of the reason for the dedication but it seems probable it was chosen as it was the name of Viscount Lifford's mother and also of several women in earlier generations of his family. The church was designed by Joseph Welland, Architect to the Ecclesiastical Commissioners.

The only extant records containing information about the original building are architectural plans and a line drawing, dated 1867, of a proposed extension. The ground plan shows the 1858 church as a small four-bay rectangular hall, with a shallow integral chancel in which the small narrow sanctuary was flanked on either side by the pulpit and reading desk. Rather curiously, given the aversion to north-facing openings in the design of many nineteenth century churches, there were three windows and a porch on the north wall of the building.

The Meenglass district was created a separate parish in 1867 and the plans for the extension, by Welland [William - son of Joseph] and Gillespie, may have been part of the preparation for the change in status of the building from chapel of ease to parish church. The plans, which adhered closely to the design of the earlier building, depict a chancel in the eastward extension to the original building and the addition of a north transept with increased seating capacity, a vestry and doorway. The new chancel was almost identical in size and layout to the one which it replaced. The drawing also shows the outline of possible further extensions with the addition of an apsidal chancel and a south transept which would have made the church cruciform in shape, but these were never built.

There is also a rudimentary outline plan, drawn in pencil, of an alternative and more limited extension proposed in 1867 by Lord Lifford. This also retained the existing church to which a small rectangular sanctuary would have been added beyond the former east wall which would be altered to form a chancel arch. This outline plan was not accepted perhaps because of the limited amount of extra seating capacity it permitted.

The extension was built to Welland and Gillespie's plans apart from a few changes made during construction to the designs of the transept gable window and the bell tower and additions to the three gable indexes. The line drawing of a north-west view of the church with the extension completed depicts dressed stone surrounds on pointed openings and on the inter-bay and angle buttresses on the walls and corners, respectively. The remainder of the walls were harled. The most decorative feature in the design for the north side was the traceried two-light window on the transept gable but when built this was a three-light stone-mullioned window. Rising from the apex of the west gable and the roof ridge, there was a short small round bell tower with a conical cap on the drawing but when built, of pitch pine, it was square shaped although retaining the conical cap above which there was an iron cross. Stone crosses surmounted the other two gables.

No photograph or written record of the interior of the church appears to have been made or kept but fortunately a parishioner recalls the building. The church was simple with central aisle and chancel, both tiled in 1910, rendered walls and an open ceiling with rendered panels between the rafters. There was no stained glass and all windows, including those on the three-light transept gable and the matching tall single lancets on the east and west gable walls, were filled with opaque lattice glazing. The baptistery, which had a simply carved rectangular font sitting on a circular shaft, was situated close to the porch door. The communion table had a simple carving of the sacred monogram IHS. The plain wooden pulpit and reading desk were located as in the 1858 building on either side of the narrow shallow sanctuary with the pulpit facing westward which meant that the preacher had his back towards those sitting in the transept. An attempt in 1910, when major repairs to the roof and floor were being carried out, to relocate the pulpit failed because it did not have the support of the non-resident Lifford family who had moved to England.

Eighteen years after it became a separate parish it was grouped with Stranorlar Parish in 1885 because of declining numbers. The debt on the extension was finally paid off in 1896 but in 1910 costly major repairs were needed and throughout the twentieth century the vestry minutes record the continuing necessary repairs. By 1957 the minutes described the church as being too large for the congregation and in a dilapidated condition requiring urgently needed repairs beyond the means of the parish.

In September 1959 Meenglass and Stranorlar parishes were united and in October 1960 plans for a new church were placed before the joint vestry. Permission to demolish the church was requested from the Sparsely Populated Area Commission of the Church of Ireland in early 1961 and later that year demolition commenced. According to some sources the building was severely damaged by Hurricane Debbie on 16 September 1961 and demolished. Local sources state however that demolition of St. Anne's had been virtually completed prior to the hurricane. It was replaced by a smaller church dedicated to The Ascension and consecrated in May 1962.

All that remains of the former St. Anne's building are a memorial wall tablet to Viscount Lifford, who died in 1887, erected by his widow Lydia Lucy, and now in the porch of the new church, the iron cross from the former bell tower now surmounting the apex of the west gable, the bell [inscribed 'presented by James Anderson' but without a date] from that tower now on the bell-gable surmounting the east gable and one of the stone crosses from the former transept or east gable, which lies, albeit cracked, on a grave in the churchyard.

Copyright R.C.B, Dublin
Meenglass: St. Anne

MONELLAN: ST. ANNE

St. Anne's, Monellan [Maigh Niallain – the plain of the little champion or of little Niall] in the Diocese of Raphoe, situated at Cross Roads village, near Killygordon, five miles west of Castlefinn, Co. Donegal, was opened for worship in 1833. It was built, with a gift of £600 from the Board of First Fruits, as a chapel of ease to the parish church of Donaghmore which was situated at Castlefinn. It has been suggested [Rowan] that it was designed 'as late as 1858' by William Armstrong of Belleek but that was the year of the consecration of St. Anne's Meenglass, situated about five miles distant. It is improbable that Armstrong designed Monellan as his year of birth, although not definitely known, is given as circa 1824 in the Irish Architectural Archive. The church is of simple three-bay rectangular hall and western tower design with architectural features typical of Board of First Fruit churches of the early nineteenth century and may have been designed by James Pain.

Unlike many other churches of that period there are window openings on both north and south walls of the hall. The original wooden frames of the Y-tracery windows on both north and south walls have been replaced over recent years with modern PVC frames with Y-tracery being retained only on those on the north wall which faces the road. The original metal framework, however, on the three-light east window has survived. All windows on the building are glazed with diamond-shaped clear glass panels.

The tower, which is integrated and supported by slim pilaster strips encasing the corners, had not been completed when the Ordnance Survey Memoir of the parish was written in 1834. It has three stages divided by string courses and is surmounted by a battlemented parapet and coping stones which are the only decorative features on the otherwise plain exterior of the building. Openings on the tower are limited to three louvred windows at the belfry stage and a porch door on the north wall facing the road. There is also a blind oculus above the porch on the middle stage perhaps indicating that it had been planned to provide a clock at some stage. The walls of tower and hall are harled with roughcast aggregate and lime and all openings are pointed and have dressed stone surrounds.

Internally the church is simple and plain with plastered walls and ceiling and a moulded cornice. There is evidence of the installation of new fittings and some alterations to the original ordering of the interior but unfortunately there are no records of those changes in the extant Vestry Minutes of 1867-1904 and 1931-1960. In keeping with other churches of the period there was no fixed baptistery in the original building. A simple limestone octagonal font with quatrefoil carvings, perhaps dating from the

Monellan, St. Anne

early twentieth century, is situated in the baptistery which now occupies one of two former box pews at the west end of the nave, one on either side of the centrally-placed aisle. The aisle, the chancel and the sanctuary are floored with tiles of different patterns and perhaps dates. The integral chancel, which occupies the full width of the hall and is raised on three tall steps, surrounds the shallow and narrow sanctuary on three sides, a feature of churches of that period.

Without records it is difficult to date the changes but some, such as the removal of the box pews and the building of a vestry at the south-east corner, may have taken place in the early 1860s, a period when many churches throughout Ireland were undergoing similar reordering. Within the sanctuary, the attractively carved reredos and communion table are the major decorative features of the interior of the church. They may have been installed in the late nineteenth or early twentieth century as a result of increasing prominence given to sacramental worship in the Church of Ireland.

On the east wall of the chancel, there is a tablet in memory of Reverend Robert Delap, curate of Donaghmore for three years and then first perpetual curate of Monellan from 1833 until his death in 1885. The church is situated in the townland of Dromore but was given the name Monellan after the townland at which the Delap family had lived for several generations in their early eighteenth century castle. This suggests that the first curate was influential in the decision to build the church. It is certain that he was a generous benefactor of the church contributing to the building fund and is recorded, in the Ordnance Survey Memoir of 1834, as having paid for the landscaping of the churchyard.

Prior to his ordination, at the age of 28, he was a barrister in Dublin. It is said that he met Daniel O'Connell at the Dublin High Court and, as a result of their conversation, promised to learn Irish from a local speaker. There was a local tradition that, before the laying out of a baptistery and installation of a font within the church, he often used a nearby stream for baptisms.

There is no extant record of the date of or reason for the dedication of the church to St. Anne. The name Anne is found in all generations of the Delap family including Robert's sister and direct female ancestors and it seems likely to have been selected by him in memory of them. He was buried in the family plot to the east of the church close to the burial ground of James, Viscount Lifford, who played a somewhat similar role in the building of St. Anne's, Meenglass, in the late 1850s.

PASSAGE EAST: ST. ANNE

Passage East, Co. Waterford, is a small village situated on the western side of the Suir Estuary, some five miles south of Waterford City. Its name comes from the Latin 'passagium', meaning a ferry. The village, which is in the parish of Kill St. Nicholas in the Diocese of Waterford, developed, as the name suggests, at the point where a ferry service across the wide estuary has operated from mediaeval times. St. Anne's Parish Church, which was closed in 1974, sold in 1978 and, since then, converted for use as a private residence, sits on a slope close to the top of a steep sandstone cliff rising above the village, coast road and estuary.

The first church on this site was an oratory, erected in 1284, 'in the name of the blessed Anne', by The Master of St. Mark's Hospital, Bristol, on land in the Manor of Coolmacsawry, a now obsolete name of an area of land to the west of Passage East. The land had been granted to him by Matthew de Bruys, a Norman settler, who, together with his wife Margery, had come from the Bristol area earlier in the century. The oratory was converted later to use as a chapel of ease in Kill St. Nicholas Parish. This building passed to the Church of Ireland at the Reformation and appears to have been used for worship until at least the middle of the seventeenth century. There is a chalice, made in London, which is dated 1641 and bears the inscription 'St. Ann's [sic] Chappell Passage'. An illustration of the area by Thomas Phillips, dated 1685, depicts the chapel to be in ruins.

The ruined chapel was replaced no later than 1730 by a new building on the same site. This may have been one of a number of churches built by Bishop Thomas Milles [1708-1740] around that time. It became the parish church and also retained the original dedication to St. Anne. It remained in use for worship throughout the eighteenth century but the fabric deteriorated gradually and a major restoration, or total rebuild according to one source, funded by a gift of £900 from the Board of First Fruits, was completed in 1817. Less than 20 years later, further repairs were needed. The repairs were funded by a grant from the Ecclesiastical Commissioners as the parish faced 'great hostility' and 'difficulties in collection of the parish cess'.

Unfortunately no photographs have been found of the exterior or interior of the building when in use for worship but it has been described as a gem of Georgian architecture. There are, however, extant architectural plans of the building, drawn by James Pain, at some time between the late 1820s and early 1840s and most likely in connection with the repairs circa 1836.

These plans show a three-bay rectangular hall with only two windows on the south wall, a narrow window on the east wall and a central aisle. An integral

Passage East, St. Anne

chancel, which occupied almost one bay, contained a centrally-positioned pulpit to the east of the altar and communion rail within the raised sanctuary. Most of the seating was of bench pews, perhaps dating from the rebuild of 1817, but some box pews had survived. The gallery at the west end extended for a short distance along both north and south walls. The church was entered by a door on the north wall of a centrally-positioned tall western porch from which steps rose to the gallery and descended to the nave.

A side elevation of the church depicting the two very tall round-headed windows on the south wall, the bell-gable surmounting the western gable wall and the substantial buttresses, somewhat similar to antae found in early Irish churches, at the eastern ends of the north and south walls, illustrates how the slope of the site was used in the internal arrangements of the church. When the church was used for worship, the bell-gable contained a small bell without date or inscription.

Considerable alterations were made to the building during the conversion to use as a private residence. At the west end, the tall porch was removed, the ground built up to gallery level and the former gallery entrance replaced by a pointed window. On the south wall, a door has been inserted at gallery level near the south west corner, a third window has been opened and the window opening on the easternmost window extended downwards to make another entrance. Unfortunately some of these alterations have been made using unsympathetic materials.

The dedication of the oratory 'in the name of the blessed Anne' in 1284 obviously resulted from the growth of the cult of the saint during that century. The dedication of the buildings in her honour remained throughout almost seven centuries during which the site was used for Christian worship. A few hundred metres to the south-east of the former church there is another feature associated with the cult of St. Anne. This was the well named St. Anne's on early Ordnance Survey maps and in early records. The well is now waterless due to the diversion of its spring. Unlike the St. Anne's Well at Killane, Co. Wexford, there is no extant record or local tradition of its use as a holy well.

RAHAN: ST. ANNE

St. Anne's, Rahan [Rahain - the ferny place], in Carrick Parish, Diocese of Kildare, was closed for worship circa 1996 and later sold. Set idyllically in over an acre of garden, now overgrown with wild flowering shrubs, beside a narrow country road in North Kildare, it is surrounded by woodland close to the entrance drive to the now vanished Palmer Estate, which covered most of Rahin [Ordnance Survey map spelling] townland. Throughout its existence, this small church remained a chapel of ease to Carbury Parish to which Carrick, never having had a parish church, was united.

According to the *Irish Builder* of 15 February 1913, the church was then in the process of construction and it was consecrated just over four months later on 24 June of that year. It was built by Charles Cauley Palmer, for his estate workers, in memory of his mother Elizabeth Anne to the design by the Orpen and Dickinson partnership, Dublin. Richard Caulfield Orpen was a pupil of Sir Thomas Deane, the famous Dublin Architect. He was also the architect of the refitting and reordering of the chancel of St. Anne's, Enniskillen, in 1923 when the parish church was raised to cathedral status and the dedication changed to St. Macartin.

The small four-bay church was a single cell building in 'neo-Hiberno Romanesque style' [Williams] with a porch, narrow vestry and organ chamber projecting from the basic rectangular shape to form a shallow cruciform outline. The roof is of Bangor blue slate and the external walls are of cut limestone with quoins at all corners and dressed stone surrounds on the bay window openings which are small, narrow and round-headed. There are two taller separated windows on each of the east and west gable walls. A narrow cornice of dressed stone runs below the eaves and the lower walls are inclined slightly outwards. In contrast to the other undecorated openings on the rest of the external walls, the porch doorway is richly decorated with columns and carved round-headed arch.

It is sad that no photographic record appears to have been made of the interior when the church was still in use for worship. Fortunately there are a few sources which contain brief descriptions. The Irish Builder stated that the furniture and fittings would be in keeping with the Romanesque style of the church. Other sources record that the distinctive carving on the porch arch was repeated on the chancel arch which was situated between the limestone ashlar walls in the nave and the Irish marble panelling in the chancel.

There were several family memorials in the church. One records that the stained glass and marble in the church were placed there by Cornelia Prime, a second cousin of Charles Cauley Palmer, in memory of her mother Anne Elizabeth Palmer. A gazetteer of Irish stained glass records that the two tall windows on the east gable were filled with glass designed and made, in 1913, by Catherine [Kitty] O'Neill of An Tur Gloine [Tower of Glass], the internationally renowned co-operative in Dublin. One of the windows was copied from Holman Hunt's famous painting, 'The Light of the World', and the other depicts Jesus as 'The Good Shepherd'. There is no record of the glazing of the other windows. The two windows by Kitty O'Neill were removed when the church was closed and are now in Carbury Parish Church, which is an appropriate place as Charles Lambe Palmer, grandfather of both Cornelia Prime and Charles Cauley Palmer, was Vicar of Carbury 1796-1840.

There is no record of the dedication of the church or the reason for the name chosen. It is would seem almost certain, however, that it was dedicated in memory of the mothers of Charles Cauley Palmer, the builder of the church, and his second cousin Cornelia Prime, the donor of the stained glass in the two east windows and the Irish marble panelling in the chancel, who were both named Anne.

This church was one of the many modest architectural treasures of the Church of Ireland which grace the Irish landscape in which they are situated. It is a shame that, prior to its closure, no proper effort was made by central church, diocesan or parish bodies to record fully this beautiful small building by word and photograph for posterity.

Rahan: St. Anne

SIXTOWNS: ST. ANNE

St. Anne's, Sixtowns, in the Diocese of Derry, is a small church, situated in the East Sperrins where the narrow mountain valley of the Moyola River begins to widen. The foundation stone was laid in March 1840 and the church, a chapel of ease to Ballynascreen [Draperstown] Parish, was consecrated on 9 August 1843. It was a trustee church with no identifiable parochial area but it served, and was located at the meeting place of, the six townlands from which it derived its name. It was built close to the old church which, according to tradition, was founded by St. Patrick and consecrated as a parish church by St. Columba.

John Stevenson, landlord of the six townlands, conveyed a piece of land in Cavanreagh townland to the Rt. Honourable Judge Robert Torrens of Derrynoyd and they, together with the Worshipful Company of Drapers and a few others, contributed the money for the erection of the building. Judge Torrens, a Justice of the Court of Common Pleas of Ireland, also made a generous endowment of £670 towards the stipend of the perpetual curate. Judge Torren's grandfather and uncle had been rectors of Ballynascreen Parish in the eighteenth century and his brother was the Archdeacon of Dublin.

There is no extant record of the reason for the dedication to St. Anne but it seems most likely that it was given that name in memory of Judge Torren's wife. There is a memorial tablet in Ballynascreen Parish Church to Anne, his 'beloved and lamented wife', who, died on 31st May 1832, aged 43. John Stevenson's wife, Rebecca, who died in 1842, is commemorated on the only wall memorial in Sixtowns Church.

The first curate, Thomas de Vere Coneys, who had been professor of Irish at T.C.D, preached in Irish and English at his first service during which hymns in both languages were sung by the 80 people in the congregation. He was succeeded in 1745 by Revd. Robert King, a noted Ulster Irish scholar, who has been called the father of modern Irish church history. The fabric of the church deteriorated during the curacy of his successor and was reported in the press, in 1874, as having been in a state of 'considerable disrepair' for some time although the Rural Dean's Visitation report of 1870 had made no reference to the condition of the church. Extensive renovations were required in 1874 including pointing of the tower, major repairs to the east wall and refurbishment of the interior structure. It was closed again in 1878 for redecoration and staining of the wooden fittings.

It is a small church with a three-bay rectangular hall and west tower of random rubble with quoins at the angles and pointed openings with dressed stone surrounds. The hall is lit on both sides by three lancet windows, at the east end by a triple lancet window, and high on the west gable by a very narrow short lancet on either side of the centrally-placed tower, all glazed with square panes of clear glass in original iron frames.

The very slightly stepped small tower, which is the most decorated part of the church exterior, has three stages divided by thin dressed stone string-courses. There are single lancets on the south, now blind, and west faces and a door on the north face while on the second stage there are distinctive short and narrow triple light windows on three faces. The belfry stage, which contains a bell without date or inscription, has louvred openings on all four faces and the tower is topped with a dressed stone band of blind arcades and a parapet surmounted by pinnacles.

Sixtowns, St. Anne

Apart from a few very minor changes, it would seem that the interior of St. Anne's remains much as it was when consecrated in 1843. The original box pews, which provide accommodation for a congregation of one hundred, have survived apart from a little alteration to the high box pews at the west end. These pews, which have wooden panelling around the walls, may have been used by the gentry. One of them now serves as a vestry. There is an elliptically shaped widening of the centrally- positioned aisle in which a pot bellied stove was originally placed with a pipe leading to a chimney in the roof. A simply carved limestone font with an octagonal shaft, the origin and date of installation of which are unknown, now stands at this place in the aisle. The raised integral chancel contains a narrow sanctuary flanked by the reading desk, entered from the sanctuary, and pulpit on the east wall. The carving on the communion rail is the only decoration on otherwise simple plain fittings.

The original flag stones remain in the aisle beneath the current covering of carpet. The walls, which have a cornice, are plastered and the plaster ceiling and roof are carried on simple roof trusses which rest on the nave walls. The church, which has no electricity, is lit by four large oil lamps.

St. Anne's is a truly delightful small early Victorian church which has fortunately escaped the ravages of time and weather and apparently the 'would be' improvers of later years. Sadly, however, the parishioners and congregations of yesteryear have gone. The 1870 Visitation Report recorded 118 parishioners and congregations of 40 and 25 at the 12.00 noon and 5.00pm services, respectively, but today there are no parishioners living in the six townlands it was built to serve. The final regular service, held monthly, ceased in October 1991. There are now just three services held each year, a Harvest Festival in October, a Christmas Carol Service in December and a service in June for the Friends of St. Anne's, which was established by the present rector in 2003.

TOEM: ST. ANNE

The parish of Toem, also known as Toomaverige and Tome Iverigg in early records, is situated in Co. Tipperary. In Gaelic it is Tuaim Ibhfeirg which is usually translated as 'the tumulus or grave of wrath' although that is disputed by some scholars. The parish, now in the Diocese of Cashel but formerly in Emly, is narrow in shape and runs from the Slieve Felim Mountains down to the fertile Golden Vale.

The earliest extant record of the parish is dated 1302 when it was claimed as part of his diocese by the Bishop of Emly, one of whose successors made it a mensal parish. Local tradition suggests that the now ruined parish church in the tiny village of Toem in the townland of Kilbeg [Cille Beag – the little church] might have been built on the site of an ancient priory.

The church may have been one of the twelve churches stated to be in repair in the Royal Visitation Report, 1615, but according to the Down Survey of 1657 it was in ruins. It was restored sometime between 1661 and 1667 and was reported as being in good repair in 1670. It was rebuilt, circa 1695, by John White of Cappaghwhite but throughout the eighteenth and early nineteenth centuries Rural Deanery Reports show the building had a chequered career. In 1788 it was in a 'ruinous condition' and by 1801 it was 'a complete ruin'. It was restored yet again, this time by private subscription and parochial assessment, and in 1808 was in perfect order but by 1832 it was in a dilapidated condition and Divine Services were being held at Cappagh House, the home of the White family at Cappaghwhite.

The Ecclesiastical Commissioners Survey of 1835 stated it was reputed to be one of the oldest church buildings of its class in use in Ireland but had fallen into ruin because of non-payment of cess. Although the church could seat 130 there were only 76 Protestants in the parish, of whom a number were families of Cornish miners brought to work in the local metal mines in the 1820s.

The church at Toem was the parish church for a group of small parishes in the area and it was decided in 1834 that, as it was ruinous and inconveniently situated, a new parish church was to be built in the village of Cappaghwhite. This decision was not implemented and the c.1695 church at Toem was rebuilt at a cost of £900 after 1837, although in that year Lewis stated it was small and dilapidated and that a new church was being contemplated.

A new church was built at Rathvyra townland in adjoining Donohill Parish in 1856. For several years services continued at Toem Church but gradually it was used less and the last service, a baptism, took place in 1886. The Diocesan Council decided, in 1887, to dismantle the building as it was considered that Donohill Church could accommodate all parishioners in the group. The nave was demolished in 1890 and the tower, which was left standing, is now a conspicuous object in the landscape.

Traces of the nave walls remain outlining a small building which was entered by a doorway on the north wall of the tower. There is some evidence on the east wall of the tower to suggest that there was a gallery at the west end of the nave. Below the outline of the roof on the same wall, there is an opening which was probably the entrance doorway to the gallery. Beneath that again on the wall there are holes in the masonry where gallery support beams would have been situated. Since demolition in 1890 the nave has been used as a burial place.

Toem: St. Anne

The three-stage western tower was not integrated in the west wall of the nave. Most of it is built of random rubble rendered and with roughly dressed quoins in places. It appears to have survived from the 1695 rebuilding and perhaps even retained at that date from the pre-1615 mediaeval building. The final two metres of the tower are of limestone ashlar, panelled in places and surmounted by a cornice and four octagonal finials of the same stone. This part of the tower was added at the time of rebuilding in the late 1830s. One corner of that addition to the tower collapsed or became dangerous and was pulled down in the twentieth century. There are openings on each stage of the tower but the only dressed stone surrounds are on the north facing doorway and window at the second stage. These are of the same stone as the upper part of the tower and were probably added in the 1830s.

It is possible that the dedication to St. Anne is a survival from the mediaeval church but there is no record of that in any of the extant early sources. There was no restoration or rebuilding during the reign of Queen Anne so it is unlikely to have been named in her memory. Another possibility is that it was named in memory of the mother of John White, who rebuilt the church in 1695, but there is no extant record of her name. The oldest headstone in the churchyard carries an inscription in memory of Susanna, wife of John White, who died in 1700.

WATERFORD CATHEDRAL: ST. ANNE'S CHAPEL

The thirteenth century cathedral at Waterford was built on the site of an earlier place of Christian worship, which may have been a cathedral of Viking origin. The nave of the mediaeval cathedral was completed in 1210 to which the chancel was added in 1220. Side aisles, each divided from the nave by an arcade of pointed arches supporting the clerestory and resting on clustered columns, were added at a later date. The ground floor stage of a large and tall tower extended from the middle bays on the north side of the building. The upper stage of the tower was surmounted by Irish stepped battlements above which rose a very low pyramidal spire.

A small chapel was built in 1482 on the north wall to the east of the tower. This chapel, dedicated to St. James the Elder and St. Catherine but eventually known as Rice's Chapel, was the gift of James Rice, a mayor of the city of Waterford for several years. The Chapter House and a later chapel stood on either side of Rice's Chapel. Other chapels, one of which was dedicated to St. Anne, were added later to the cathedral by wealthy citizens and businessmen of Waterford but there is no extant record of the locations of St. Anne's or the other chapels within the building.

The cult of St. Anne had spread originally to Ireland after the Norman invasion in the late twelfth century and was maintained in the area by the strong links between Waterford and Bristol and the west of England. An oratory dedicated to St. Anne had been established in 1284 at Passage East, a few miles to the south of Waterford.

The date of the building of the St. Anne Chapel is not known but it was certainly prior to the Reformation when the cathedral passed to the Church of Ireland which abolished the practice by the mediaeval church of building side chapels with altars. The actual date of dedication of the chapel to St. Anne is not known but it must have taken place when the cult associated with the saint was at its zenith in Ireland during the very late fifteenth and early sixteenth centuries. The Chapel existed as part of the Church of Ireland Cathedral from the Reformation until the mediaeval structure was unfortunately demolished in 1773.

BIBLIOGRAPHY

Akenson, D.H., *The Church of Ireland: Ecclesiastical reform and revolution 1800-1885*, New Haven, 1971

Allingham, H., *Ballyshannon: Its History and Antiquities*, Londonderry, 1879

Annals of Killane Parish, MS compiled by Cooper, A.W.F., Rector 1898-1921, and his successors, nd.

Ashley, K. and Scheingorm, P., (eds), *Interpreting Cultural Symbols: St. Anne in Late Mediaeval Society*, London, 1990

Benn, G., *A History of the town of Belfast......*, Belfast, 1823

Binions, G., *Rathnure and Killanne: A History*, Killanne, 1997

Bowe, N.G., Caron, D. and Wynne, M., *Gazetteer of Irish Stained Glass*, Dublin, 1998

Brandon, E.A., *To whom we are dedicated*, Dundalk, 1954

Bradshaw, W.H., *Enniskillen Long Ago: an Historic Sketch of the Parish, Church and Town*, Dublin, 1878

Brady, W.M., *Clerical and Parochial Records of Cork, Cloyne and Ross*, Dublin, 1864

Brett, C.E.B., *Buildings of Belfast, 1700-1914*, Belfast, 1967

Brett, C.E.B., *Historic Buildings, Groups of Buildings and Areas of Architectural Importance in the towns and villages of East Down*, Belfast, 1974

Brooking, C., *The City of Dublin*, London, 1728

Butler, D.J., *Journal of the Royal Society of Antiquaries of Ireland, Vol.134*, Dublin, 2004

Carlow Sentinel, 30 April 1842

Casey, C., *Dublin*, Dublin, 2005

Casey, C. and Rowan, A.J., *The Buildings of North Leinster*, London, 1993

Clark, M. and Refausse, R., *Directory of Historic Dublin Guilds*, Dublin, 1993

Cole, J.H., *Church and Parish Records of the United Dioceses of Cork, Cloyne and Ross of the forty years from A.D. 1863*, Cork, 1903

Comerford, R.V., and others, (eds), *Religion, Conflict and Coexistence in Ireland*, Dublin, 1990

Costello, P., *Dublin Churches*, Dublin, 1989

Craig, M., *Dublin 1600-1810*, London, 1982

Crawford, J., *Within Thy Walls, the story of St. Audoen's Church, Cornmarket, Dublin*, Dublin, 1986

Crooks, D.W.T., *Living Stones*, _____, 2001

Cross, F.L. and Livingstone, E.A ., (eds), *The Oxford Dictionary of the Christian Church*, Oxford, 2005

Crowley, J.S., Devoy, R.J.N., Linehan, D. and O'Flanagan,P., *Atlas of Cork City*, Cork, 2005

Day, A. and McWilliams, P., (eds), *Ordnance Survey Memoirs of Ireland*, Belfast, 1990-1998

Dixon, H., *An Introduction to Ulster Architecture*, Belfast, 1975

Dixon, H., *U.A.H.S. List of Historic Buildings, Groups of Buildings and Areas of Architectural Importance in the town of Enniskillen*, Belfast, 1973

Dundas, E.T., *A Short History of Kilbarron Parish*, _____, nd

Dundas, W.H., *Enniskillen, Parish and Town*, Dundalk, 1913

Dunlop, D., (ed), *A Memoir of the professional Life of William J. Barre*, Belfast, 1868

Dukes, F.E., *Campanology in Ireland*, Dublin, 1994

Dukes, F.E., *Notes on church bells*, R.C.B. Library, Dublin

Erck, J.C., *The Irish Ecclesiastical Register for the years 1817, 1818, 1820, 1825 and 1830*, Dublin

Fawcett, F.W. and Crooks, D.W.T., (eds), *Clergy of Derry and Raphoe*, Belfast, 1999

Forrester, L., *Easkey Church Restoration Appeal Literature*, unpublished, nd,

Galloway, P., *The Cathedrals of Ireland*, Belfast, 1992

Gebbie. J., *In His Hand*, _____, 1970

Gilbert, J.T., *Calendar of Ancient Records of Dublin*, Dublin, 1720-1 [reprinted 1894]

Gilbert, J.T., *History of the City of Dublin*, Dublin, 1861

Godkin, J., *Ireland and her Churches*, London, 1867

Hardy, P.D., (ed), *Twenty One Views in Belfast and its Neighbourhood*, Dublin, 1837

Healy, E., *In Search of Ireland's Holy Wells*, Dublin, 2001

His Majesty's Commissioners on Ecclesiastical Revenue and Patronage, First Report 1834, Second Report 1835, Third Report 1836 and Fourth Report 1838, London

Hutchison, S., *Towers, Spires and Pinnacles*, Bray, 2003

Journals of the House of Commons of the Kingdom of Ireland, 1613-1800, 19 vols, Dublin, 1795-1800 [reprinted with index 1802]

Kelly, L., Lucid, G. and O'Sullivan, M., *Blennerville: Gateway to Tralee's Past*, Tralee, 1989

Joyce, P.W., *Irish Place Names*, Dublin, 1913

Knox. T.K., *Notes on the Early History of Tuam, Killala and Achonry*, Dublin, 1904.

Larmour, P., *Belfast: An Illustrated Architectural Guide*, Belfast, 1987

Leslie, J.B., *Ardfert Clergy and Parishes*, Dublin, 1940

Leslie, J.B., *Armagh Clergy and Parishes*, Dundalk, 1911

Leslie, J.B., *Clogher Clergy and Parishes*, Enniskillen, 1929

Leslie, J.B., *Derry Clergy and Parishes*, Enniskillen, 1937

Leslie, J.B., *Ferns Clergy and Parishes*, Dublin, 1936

Leslie, J.B., *Raphoe Clergy and Parishes*, Enniskillen, 1940

Leslie, J.B., *Ardagh Clergy Succession list*, unpublished Ms, nd

Leslie, J.B., *Elphin Clergy Succession list*, unpublished Ms, nd

Leslie, J.B., *Kildare Clergy Succession list*, unpublished Ms, nd

Leslie, J.B., *Killala Clergy Succession list*, unpublished Ms, nd

Leslie, J.B., *Leighlin Clergy Succession list*, unpublished Ms, nd

Lewis, S., *A Topographical Dictionary of Ireland*, London, 1837

Logan, P., *The Holy Wells of Ireland*, Buckinghamshire, 1980

Mackey, P., *Selected walks through Old Waterford*, Waterford, 1984

McKnight, T.R., *The Little Church in the Valley, St. Anne's, Sixtowns*, _____, 1983

McMahon, M., *St. Audoen's Church, Cornmarket, Dublin: Archaeology and Architecture*, Dublin, 2006

Monteith, E.W., *A History of Drumglass Parish*, Dungannon, c.1967.

Moore, M.J., *Archaeological Inventory of Leitrim*, Dublin, 2003

Moore, M.J., *Archaeological Inventory of Waterford*, Dublin, 1999

Moore, M.J., *Archaeological Inventory of Wexford*, Dublin, 1996

Mottram, P., *John Macduff Derick: A biographical sketch, Ecclesiology Today, no.32*, London, 2004.

O'Ceallaigh, S., (ed), *Aspects of our rich inheritance: Cloghaneely*, _____, 2000

O'Concubhar, P., *A Visionary Enthusiast: Robert Emmet and his Kerry connections*, Blennerville (?), 2003 (?)

O'Dwyer, F., *Architecture of Deane and Woodward*, Cork, 1997

Paterson, J.T.F., *Historical Guide to Meath and Kildare*, Kingscourt, 1981

Potterton, H., *Irish Church Monuments 1570-1880*, Belfast, 1975

Power, D., *Archaeological Inventory of North Cork*, Dublin, 2000

Power, P., *The Place Names of Decies*, London, 1907

Poyntz, S.G., *St. Ann's: The church in the heart of the city*, Dublin, 1967

Rankin, F., and others, *Clergy and Parishes of Down and Dromore*, Belfast, 1996

Rennison, W.H., *Succession list of the bishops, cathedral and parochial clergy of the dioceses of Waterford and Lismore*, Ardmore, 1920

Richardson, D.S., *Gothic Revival Architecture in Ireland*, New York, 1983

Robbins, N., *An exact abridgement of all Irish statutes in force in Ireland and relating to Ecclesiastical matters from the Magna Carta to 14th year of the reign of His Majesty King George II,* Dublin, 1741

Ronan, M.V., *St. Anne: Her Cult and her shrines*, London, 1927

Rowan, A.J., *North West Ulster*, London, 1979

Ryan, A., *Toemverig Toom, Toem*, Cappawhite, 1992

St. Anne's Church of Ireland, Knocknarea, Co. Sligo, unpublished Ms, 1991(?)

Seymour, St. J.D., *The Diocese of Emly*, Dublin, 1913

Seymour, St. J.D., *Notes on a Tipperary Parish, Cork Historical and Archaeological Journal, vol. xiii,* Cork, 1917

Seymour, St. J.D., *The Succession of Parochial Clergy in the United Diocese of Cashel and Emly,* Dublin, 1908

Seymour, St. J.D., *Church Plate and Parish Records of Cashel and Emly*, Clonmel, 1930

Shaw, H., *Dublin pictorial guide and directory of 1850*, Dublin, 1850

Smith, C., *The antient and present state of the county and city of Cork*, Dublin, 1774

Smith, C., *The antient and present state of the county of Kerry*, Dublin, no date

Smith, C., *The antient and present state of the county and city of Waterford*, Dublin, 1774

The Builder, August 28th 1858, London

Trimble, W.C., *The history of Enniskillen with reference to some manors in Co. Fermanagh*, Enniskillen, 1919-21

Tuckey, J., *200 years of Bells of Shandon 1752-1952*, Cork, 1952

Vestry Minutes of the parishes of Blennerville, Castlemartyr, St. Ann's, Dawson St., Dublin, Kilglass and Killane – held at RCB Library, Dublin: Drumglass and Killult – held at PRONI, Belfast: Monellan and Meenglass– held in local custody.

Wagner, W.E., *History and Succession List of Clergy of Elphin*, unpublished Ms, nd

Walker, B.M. and Dixon, H., *In Belfast Town: 1864-1880:* Belfast, 1984

Walker, B.M. and Dixon, H., *No Mean City: Belfast 1880-1914, in the photographs of Robert French*, Belfast, 1983

Walker, S., *Historic Ulster Churches*, Belfast, 2000

Walton, J.C., *Decies, vol 12, 1979*, Waterford, 1979

Walton, J.C., *Irish Genealogist, vol. 4, no. 4, November, 1971*, Dublin, 1971

Ware, Sir J., *The whole works of Sir James Ware concerning Ireland........ revised and improved ... in two volumes*, Dublin, 1764

Webster, C.A., *Church Plate of Cork, Cloyne and Ross*, Cork, 1909

Webster, C.A., *The Diocese of Cork*, Cork, 1920

Wheeler, H.A. and Craig, M., *The Dublin City Churches of the Church of Ireland*, Dublin, 1948

Williams, J., *A Companion Guide to Architecture of Ireland 1837-1921*, Dublin, 1994

Winnett, A., *Peter Brown, provost, bishop and metaphysician*, London, 1971

Young, J.A., *Unfinished pilgrimage: the story of Belfast Cathedral*, Belfast, c.1960

GLOSSARY

AEDICULE   an opening framed by a pair of columns or pilasters and surmounted by a pediment

AISLE   a passageway running parallel to the main span of the church and also a lateral extension of a nave but separated from it by an arcade

ALABASTER   gypsum used in fittings and monuments as it was easily carved

ALTAR   table used for Celebration of the Eucharist, also called the Communion Table

AMBULATORY   an aisle surrounding a chancel on three sides

ANTAE   a prolongation or extension of side walls beyond the gable wall

APSE   a projection, normally polygonal or semicircular in shape and often vaulted, extending from the walls of a church

ARCADE   a series of arches supported by piers or columns: termed BLIND when the intervening spaces are closed

ARCH   a curved series of wedge shaped blocks which carry the weight of the structure above

ARTS and CRAFTS   an artistic movement which developed c.1870-1914 as a response to mass production and sought to revive hand made objects of simple design

AN TUR GLOINE   The Tower of Glass, a co-operative of Irish stained glass artists which was an important part of the Celtic Art and Crafts Movement in the early twentieth century and acquired a deserved international reputation

ASHLAR   large blocks of masonry cut, dressed and squared

BALUSTER   a short pillar or post standing on a base and supporting a rail or coping

BALUSTRADE   a series of balusters supporting a rail or coping: termed BLIND when set against a wall

BAPTISTERY   the part of the church in which baptism is administered

BATTLEMENT   a parapet with indentations (embrasures) and raised sections (merlons) and an IRISH BATTLEMENT where the parapet builds up in steps to the corners

BATTER   an inclined face of a wall

BAY   a vertical division of a building defined by regular features such as windows, columns or arches

BELFRY   a structure in which bells are housed

BELL-GABLE   a vertical projection with opening above the gable end of the church which carries a small bell

BELL LOUVRE   a window shaped opening in the belfry wall of a tower in which horizontal, overlapping and sloping wooden slats exclude rain and permit the sound of the bells to be heard

BOARD OF FIRST FRUITS   first fruits, originally called annates, were the first year's revenue of a benefice and a small proportion of all future years' revenues which were paid to the papacy and, after the Reformation, to the Crown. First Fruits were remitted to the Church of Ireland during the reign of Queen Anne and a Board was set up in 1711 to administer the funds mainly for the purchase, building and repair of glebe houses. From 1777 onwards the government augmented the funds of the board and money was spent increasingly on building and repairing churches. Without the loans and grants from the Board many country churches would not have been built

BOX PEW   pews enclosed by high panelled timber partitions with hinged doors

BROACHED SPIRE   an octagonal spire resting on a square tower without a parapet and contained by semi pyramidal wedges at the corners

BUTTRESS   vertical structures projecting from a wall or at corners of a building to give added strength or provide decorative features

CANOPY   a projection or hood over an opening or a niche

CAPITAL   the head or top part of a column, pier or pilaster

CHAMFER   the surface of a stone or timber feature formed by cutting off a squared edge

CHANCEL   the eastern portion of the church which included the choir, clergy and sanctuary and was typically shorter, narrower and lower: in the majority of the hall churches built in the seventeenth and eighteenth centuries the chancel was integral being contained within in the main body of the building

CHANCEL ARCH   arched opening providing access from the nave, the main body of the church, to the chancel

CHANTRY   a chapel with an endowment for the chanting of masses usually for the souls of the founders of the endowment

CHAPEL OF EASE   a church built to serve the needs of a growing population in an area or parishioners living several miles distant from the parish church

CHAPTER HOUSE   a building used for meetings of the cathedral chapter, the canons of the cathedral

CLERESTORY   upper storey, pierced by windows, in the main walls of a building

COLONETTE   small column or shaft

COLONNADE   a range of columns supporting arches or an entabulature

CORBEL   a projecting stone, often carved with angels, supporting the weight of a feature resting upon it: CORBEL STOP   carved projection at the termination of a corbel: CORBEL TABLE   a row of projecting stones supporting a projection such as a moulded course or a parapet

COLUMN   a vertical cylindrical pillar used for structural support or adornment

COPING   a course of stones resting on the top of a wall providing a protective cap which disperses rain water

CORNICE   an ornamental moulding projecting from the upper reaches of an external wall or in the angle where the interior wall and ceiling meet

COMMUNION RAIL   a rail introduced after the Reformation to protect the communion table

CROCKET   a carved feature, usually in the shape of leaves, first introduced in Gothic buildings, and placed at regular intervals on the sloping sides of spires, pinnacles and gables

CROSSING   the space where nave/chancel and transept axes meet

CROW STEPPED   stepped slope of a gable wall

CRUCIFORM   church built in the shape of a cross with transepts

CUPOLA   a small circular or polygonal dome crowning a roof or tower

COURSE   a continuous single horizontal row or layer of stones or bricks in a wall

DECORATED   English Gothic Architecture c.AD1290-c.1350

DRESSED STONE   smoothly finished stone used in architectural features such as window openings, doorways, quoins and string courses

DRIPSTONE   moulded stone projecting from a wall, especially over door and window openings, to protect the lower walls from water

EARLY ENGLISH   English Gothic Architecture c.AD1200-c.1250

EAVES   the lower part of a sloping roof which overhangs a wall

ECCLESIASTICAL COMMISSIONERS   the successors to the Board of First Fruits, established to make improvements in the Church of Ireland using the money made available by the suppression, under the Church Temporalities Act of 1833, of two archbishoprics, ten bishoprics and clergy sinecures and the reduction of the incomes of several bishoprics

ELEVATION   a side of a building represented in a two dimensional drawing

ENTABLATURE   the collective name given in classical architecture to a decorated band consisting of the three moulded horizontal features – cornice, frieze, architrave – above a column

FAÇADE   the front or face of a building

FINIAL   a carved ornament on top of a canopy, cupola, gable, pinnacle or spire

FLUTING   shallow concave grooves running vertically on the shaft of a pillar or column

FOIL   decorative feature in a space formed by the cusping in an opening or panel

GABLE   the upper part of the wall, usually peaked and triangular in shape, supporting the end of a ridged roof: GABLET a small gable

GALLERY   an upper storey providing additional tiered seating overlooking the nave

GARGOYLE   a water spout projecting from the main building and often carved in grotesque human or animal shapes

GIBBSIAN   the use of shallow projecting squared blocks of stone of alternating lengths surrounding door and window openings

GLEBE   land which belonged to the Established Church and formed part of the income of the incumbent and on part of which a glebe house was built

GOTHIC REVIVAL   any use of Gothic after the classical period

GUILD   a religious fraternity, professing devotion to a saint, whose members often worked together in a craft or trade and endowed a chantry or chapel

HAMMERBEAM   horizontal brackets of a roof projecting at wall plate level similar to a tie beam with the middle section removed

HARLED   roughcast render on a wall with sand, lime, and small gravel

HIBERNO-ROMANESQUE   style of church building in Ireland c.AD1000-c.1300

HOOD MOULD   a projecting moulding on the face of a wall above an arch, door or window

KING POST   the central vertical post rising from a tie beam to the ridge piece

LABEL   see dripstone and hood moulding

LABEL STOP   carved decorative feature at the termination of a label, hood moulding or string course

LANCET   a slender window with a pointed head and no tracery

LECTERN   reading stand to hold a copy of the Bible

LIGHT   separate component part of a window

LINTEL   a horizontal beam or stone spanning an opening

LOMBARDIC   a style of architecture c.AD1300-c.1400 from Lombardy in Italy

LOUVRE   see bell louvre

LUCARNE   a small opening on a spire, usually decorative and often capped with a gable and finial

MOSAIC   a picture or pattern created using small coloured pieces of glass or stone

MOULDING   a feature of continuous section

MULLIONS   a vertical post or upright dividing an opening with lights into separate compartments

NARTHEX   an enclosed vestibule at the main entrance to a church often extending across the west end

NAVE   the western section of a church often extended laterally by addition of one or more aisles

NICHE   a recess in a wall or reredos often containing a statue or a decorative feature

OCULUS   a circular opening or recess in a wall

ORATORY   a place of worship other than a parish church and in mediaeval times often built at remote and inaccessible areas of large parishes

ORIENTATION   tradition has it that mediaeval churches were built with the chancel to the east facing Jerusalem but in some places the site made an eastern orientation impossible requiring the building to be reversed although the architectural features, eg., west front, of such buildings are nevertheless described as being orientated correctly

OXFORD MOVEMENT   a nineteenth century movement in the Church of England aimed at restoring high church principles and architectural features at a time of increasing theological liberalism

PANELLING   a decorative pattern applied to a blank surface usually of wood but occasionally stone

PARAPET   a wall, which may be plain, battlemented, pierced or carved, for protection at any sudden drop or to conceal guttering

PATRON SAINT   a saint in whose honour a church is dedicated, but in mediaeval times a saint who was also the special intercessor in heaven of an individual or body such as a church or guild

PEDIMENT   a low pitched gable used in Classical and Renaissance architecture above a portico, door, window or niche, called BROKEN where the horizontal base is incomplete and OPEN where the apex is omitted

PERPENDICULAR   the last of the Gothic architectural styles c.AD.1400-c.1450

PERPETUAL CURATE   a priest appointed to serve in a chapel of ease or a district church

PIERS   a column or other support dividing the nave or chancel from an aisle, called COMPOUND when formed of a number of shafts

PILASTER   a shallow rectangular column attached to a wall: called a PILASTER STRIP where the column has no base or capital

PINNACLE   a miniature spire, often ornamented with crockets, built as a decorative termination to a buttress, parapet angle, or turret

PORCH   an architectural feature protecting the entrance to a church

PORTICO   a covered space, open on at least one side and delimited by a colonnade which supports the roof and often a pediment

POLYCHROMATIC   the use of stone of several colours usually for external decoration

QUARRY GLASS   one of a series of small panels of glass usually diamond or square shaped

QUEEN POST   one of two vertical posts rising from the tie beam to the collar beam of a queen post roof

QUOINS   interlocking stones of alternating length, usually dressed, forming the angle of a building

RECUSANT   a person who refused to submit to the authority and attend services of the established church

RENDERING   process of covering walls with a skin of varying materials and in the case of exterior walls to protect them from the weather

REREDOS   a decorative stone or wooden screen covering the wall above and behind the altar or communion table

REVEAL   inward plane of the side surface between the edge of a wall and the frame of the door or window

ROMANESQUE   the style of architecture prevalent in Europe c.AD900-c.1200 which preceded Gothic and was characterised by round headed door and window openings

ROSE WINDOW   circular window, usually found on gable walls, with complex tracery similar in pattern to the petals of a rose

RUBBLE   walling of rough or unsquared stones but term does not infer inferior masonry: where laid in a random uncoursed pattern it is called RANDOM RUBBLE

SANCTUARY   area around the altar or communion table usually surrounded by a communion rail

SHAFT   the part of a column or pier between the base and capital

SHINGLE   wooden tile used in covering roofs, spires and walls

SPIRE   a tall pyramidal or conical feature built on a tower or turret

SQUINT   an opening cut through an internal wall to enable priests to see the sanctuary

STEEPLE   a tower surmounted by a spire

STRING-COURSE   an elevated projecting horizontal band, normally moulded, on a wall

THREE-DECKER   a fitting in post-Reformation Anglican churches containing a pulpit, reading desk and parish clerk's desk on three descending levels: usually situated at the east end of the church reflecting the increased emphasis in worship on the Word at that period

TIE BEAM   the horizontal transverse beam in a roof tying together the feet of rafters

TOWER   usually situated at the west end of the church it may be composed of two or more floors, called stages, often delineated by string courses and may be stepped, when the succeeding stages are reduced in area

TRACERY   the pattern of ornamental open stonework in the upper part of Gothic windows: called BLIND TRACERY when applied to walls

TRACTARIAN   a movement within the Anglican church in the nineteenth century stressing its links with Catholic Christianity

TRANSEPT   a transverse part, or arm, of a cruciform shaped church

TREFORIUM   the middle tier of a church interior with the nave arcade below and the clerestory above

TRUSS   timber supporting a roof

TURRET   a small tower often with a staircase providing access to the tower

TYMPANUM   a triangular or semi circular surface between the lintel of a doorway or window and the arch above it

VAULTING   an arched ceiling

VESTIBULE   an entrance hall or anteroom

VESTRY   an Anglican term for sacristy where sacred vessels and vestments are kept

Photo Gallery

Annaduff: St. Ann

Belfast Cathedral: St. Anne

Castlemartyr: St. Anne

Cork, Shandon: St Anne

Easkey: St. Anne

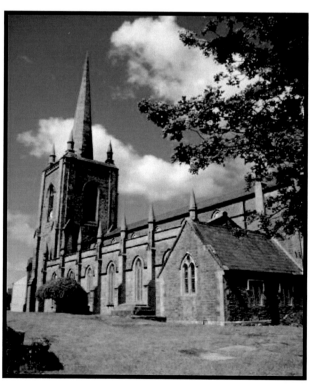

Enniskillen: St. Anne (now St. Macartin)

Kilbarron: St. Anne

Killult: St. Ann

Knocknarea: St. Anne

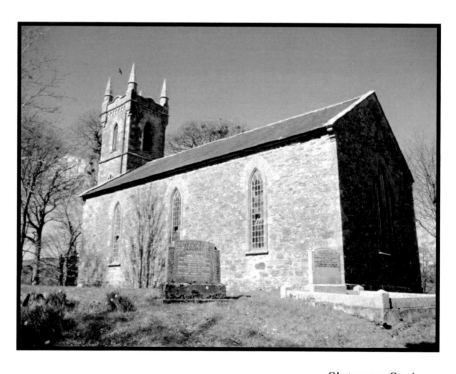

Sixtowns: St. Anne